THE GOAL MACHINE

THE GOAL MACHINE

Portrait of a Football Superstar

JASON TOMAS

MAINSTREAM
PUBLISHING

EDINBURGH AND LONDON

First published in 1997 by
MAINSTREAM PUBLISHING COMPANY
(EDINBURGH) LTD
7 Albany Street
Edinburgh EH1 3UG

ISBN 1 85158 927 9

A catalogue record for this book is available from the
British Library

Photographs © Empics
Graphics by Roy Cooper

Typeset in Bembo
Printed and bound in Great Britain by Butler & Tanner Ltd

Contents

CHAPTER ONE

Written in the Stars

Martine Delamere admits that she knows 'eff-all' about football and the game's leading lights. All she knows about Alan Shearer is what she saw of him when, like millions of others who don't normally follow the game, she tuned in to England's Euro 96 matches on TV. As one of Britain's foremost astrologers, however, she does not need to have much knowledge of Shearer's football career to provide a profound insight into why he has become Britain's most respected player.

Delamere is an expert at assessing the psychological make-up of people, their characters and personalities, on information derived on their star signs and the relative positions of the sun, moon and various planets at the time they were born. Some might scoff at this 'science'; a number still cling to the vision of astrology at the superficial level presented by the Gypsy Rose Lees of British holiday resort fame, and newspaper and magazine star-sign columns.

With the right information, Delamere can be rather more penetrative and specific. Indeed, her ability to unravel what lies inside people, and advise them on how their abilities can best be applied to enable them to fulfil their potential, has attracted clients from all walks of life, from private individuals to celebrities and even major corporations.

If you believe that the path people follow in life can be written in the stars, then Alan Shearer makes as fascinating a subject for such analysis as anybody. Quite apart from his ability as a striker, which has twice earned him the accolade of Player of the Year from his fellow professionals, his personality and temperament have helped make him the most popular English footballer since Gary Lineker. He is more noticeably combative and abrasive than Lineker was but, like the former Leicester, Everton and Tottenham player, his public image is little short of blemish-free.

For those in the public eye, there is a lot to be said, financially, for being seen to be respectable and decent. In an interview with Neil Harman of the *Daily Mail*, it was suggested to Shearer that this side of him – his boy-next-door image – was manufactured. 'There is a suspicion that he doesn't say controversial things because he has been groomed by the kind of PR machine that kept Lineker squeaky clean until his recent biography was published,' wrote Harman.

Shearer rejected this view. 'I wouldn't dream of criticising any-one in public, and I also think it is part of my responsibilities to look clean and respectable when I'm in front of a camera repres-enting myself, my club or England,' he said. 'I know that kids can be swayed by the impression footballers give. It's important we look the part.'

In another interview, with Steven Howard in *The Sun* in May 1997, Shearer gave an even more refreshing view of his mentality: 'I look at my bank balance and think what a lucky lad I am. Sometimes I reckon there are too many noughts on it. I realise fully just how fortunate I have been and I understand people outside the game saying the money I earn is absurd. People do far worthier jobs, and get nothing in comparison.' He claimed that his attitude to fame and wealth stemmed from his upbringing: 'I grew up in the North-east, in a family where both my mum and dad worked and still do. My mum is a part-time home help, while my dad is a sheet-metalworker. He started at 16 and he's 53 now. He's away at half six in the morning, not back until seven at night, and still does two nights a week overtime.'

All this, combined with the fact that Shearer also looks every inch a world-class footballer on the field, makes it easy to understand why he is a marketing dream.

To some extent, the reasons why this 27-year-old has progressed further than a lot of players who had superior ball-playing skills have been plain for all to see. Most people, for example, will readily endorse Martine Delamere's observation that Alan Shearer is a man who can achieve virtually anything he sets his heart on. She uses words like 'tunnel-visioned', 'driven' and 'obsessional' to describe him. That such characteristics are channelled into the scoring of goals means that he is capable of lifting teams on to the same high plateau that he reaches himself. When Shearer is on a football pitch, the one thing we can be sure of is that there are precious few situations that can be viewed by his colleagues as lost causes.

To appreciate why Shearer is the world's most expensive player – and why the £15 million Newcastle paid Blackburn for him was not as outlandish a figure as some suggested – it is important to look not just at his goals, but at the circumstances in which many of his most notable strikes have been achieved. That old catch-phrase concerning the strength of character and single-mindedness of leading sports performers – 'When the going gets tough, the tough get going' – could easily have been coined with Alan Shearer in mind.

One of the numerous teams to end up with this thought were Leicester City in the Premiership match at Newcastle on Sunday, 2 February 1997. Though lacking Newcastle's individual talent, the newly promoted Leicester had established themselves as one of the Premiership teams with the most impressive spirit and organisation. Thus, when they recovered from being one down at half-time with three goals in 14 minutes in the second half, there seemed no way back for the shell-shocked home side. But 15 minutes from the end, Shearer gave them their first glimmer of hope with a spectacular goal direct from a free-kick 25 yards out – and he went on to complete a hat-trick to earn United the most improbable of 4–3 wins.

Statistics can tell all manner of different stories. However, when viewing Shearer's scoring record for Blackburn and Newcastle – the clubs at which his development has reached its height – it is tempting to suggest that the old view about one man not making a team is considerably less true in his case than it might be in others.

Notwithstanding the scoring chances he makes for team-mates, he himself got 112 goals in 138 Premiership matches in four seasons with Blackburn (almost a half of his team's overall total) and 25 in 31 matches in his first season at Newcastle. In a campaign which saw the sensational resignation of manager Kevin Keegan, those Shearer goals – scored on either side of a period in which he underwent a third groin operation in nine months – helped the club finish in second place in the league, and clinch a place along-side Manchester United in the European Champions' League.

It is not unreasonable to suggest that had Shearer been able to play in every Newcastle match, Kenny Dalglish, his former mana-ger at Blackburn and Keegan's successor at St James's Park, would have been celebrating another Championship triumph. Newcastle won only two of the seven Premiership matches that Shearer missed; and he was also absent when they fell to Monaco in the quarter-finals of the UEFA Cup.

One extraordinary aspect of Shearer's scoring record is the extent to which he has been hampered by injury problems. The blow he suffered before the start of the 1997–98 season, when he fractured his right fibula and damaged ankle ligaments during the Umbro Cup match against Chelsea might have been softened by his experiences of such setbacks. Take his so-called 'dodgy' right knee. He had a cartilage operation while at Southampton in 1991, but much worse was to follow in his first season at Blackburn. Having responded to the challenge imposed by his then British record transfer fee of £3.3 million by scoring 22 goals in Rovers' first 21 matches, and established himself as a key figure in England's bid to qualify for the 1994 World Cup finals in the USA, Shearer had to undergo a major operation to repair cruciate ligament damage. This has become the most feared of all injuries to profes-sional footballers. Among those whose careers have been threatened by it are Paul Gascoigne, who might well feel that it was the beginning of the end for him in that he has still to recover his previous level of fitness. It was perhaps typical of Shearer that when he returned to the Blackburn first team at the start of the following season – after a recovery programme stretching some eight months – he did so looking as dynamic and effective as ever.

His scoring prowess proved particularly valuable to Rovers in the 1994–95 season, of course, when his 34 goals – including ten penalties – steered them to their first Championship in 81 years. Blackburn struggled to maintain their success the following season, but Shearer had no such problems. He scored 31 goals this time to help them finish seventh. It was during that season that Shearer became the first player to hit the 100-goal mark in the Premiership, a distinction clinched with his strike in the 2–1 win over Tottenham on 30 December 1995.

At international level, too, Shearer can always be relied upon to come shining through the most daunting of obstacles. Things were hardly looking good for him in the build-up to Euro 96, when his run of England matches without a goal had reached 12, and the coach, Terry Venables, inevitably came under increasing pressure to drop him. Typical of the reaction to this 21-month lean spell was an article by John Sadler in *The Sun*, under the headline: 'Do Shearer a big favour and drop him, Terry – Venables must be cruel to be kind'. Only two strikers had previously gone as many matches without an England goal as Shearer had – Luther Blissett (February 1983–June 1984) and Trevor Francis (September 1983–April 1986). The only one to have suffered even more was Mark Hateley, whose goal drought lasted 14 matches from June 1986 to March 1992.

Shearer's disappointing run, which began after his two goals in the 2–0 win over the USA at Wembley in September 1994 (which had taken his total to five in 11 internationals), could be easily rationalised. The England system, in which he operated up front virtually on his own, meant that much of his time – perhaps too much – was spent with his back to the opponents' goal. Instead of

11

following his natural instincts to get behind the players marking him, Shearer, often heavily outnumbered, had to concentrate more on linking up England's attacking play and creating space for other potential scorers. Moreover, in the season leading up to Euro 96, he had been troubled by a groin injury, something of an occupational hazard for footballers with his explosive physical style of play.

Venables, shrewd enough to appreciate that Shearer reacts superbly to personal challenges, and that Euro 96 was viewed by the striker as a vital stage for him on which to further his career, kept faith with the player. For his part, Shearer, increasingly struck by the feeling that he had gone as far as he could with Blackburn, was so determined to do justice to himself in Euro 96 that he even elected to take the calculated risk of undergoing an operation on the groin shortly before the end of the season. This move provoked the view in some quarters that he was being selfish. The groin trouble had not stopped him playing for Blackburn – and playing well by normal standards. Indeed, by the time he elected to withdraw from the Blackburn team two matches before the end of the season, his personal target of becoming the first player to score 30 league goals in each of three consecutive seasons had been reached, with a brace in the 3–1 win over Wimbledon. One of the problems for Blackburn in the timing of his operation was that, at that stage, they still had a chance of qualifying for the UEFA Cup. But Shearer, pointing out that he had hardly trained for 11 weeks, was quoted in the *News of the World* as saying: 'If I was motivated by personal glory, I would have delayed the operation until the end of the season to give myself a better chance of winning the Golden Boot award as the top scorer in the Premiership. As it is, I've finished on 31 goals and have given Robbie Fowler and Les Ferdinand [the next men on the highest-scorers' list] the chance to overtake me. But all this is secondary to my wish to get fully fit and free of pain. In the Premiership, you cannot get away with operating below your full fitness level for too long. For me it reached the stage where I could only run at 80 per cent speed and every time I had a shot, I was getting a sharp pain which was becoming intolerable. I know I have been scoring goals for Blackburn, but that has hidden the fact that I have been playing badly.'

Playing badly is the very last accusation that could have been levelled against the player in Euro 96. Such was his recovery from the operation that he finished the tournament as the top scorer with five goals and the kudos of being recognised as the man who had done the most in England's memorable run to the semi-finals. The timing of his goals was interesting, in that in the opening two matches, they came at moments when England were finding it difficult to establish a grip on the games. He scored the first goal in the 1–1 draw against Switzerland, and in the 2–0 win over Scotland. The lead also came from him – in more ways than one – with his 23rd-minute penalty in the astonishing 4–1 win over Holland (a match in which he scored twice) and the 1–1 draw in the semi-final against Germany.

The following season, in their first match back at Wembley for the World Cup qualifying tie against Poland, the England team, now under the management of Glenn Hoddle, looked a pale shadow of the side who had enthralled millions during the summer. Shearer by now had the added responsibility of being England captain, an honour bestowed on him through the absence of Arsenal's injured Tony Adams. It is rare for a striker to be given the skipper's job, because of the usual self-centred nature of the leading scorers and the fact that they do not see enough of the full picture of a match to be able to concern themselves effectively with what is happening in other departments of their teams.

But Alan Shearer is no ordinary striker; he scored the goals that enabled England to beat the Poles 2–1, after going a goal down. In the return tie in Chorzow on 1 June 1997, England, pushed into second place in the group after losing 1–0 to Italy at Wembley, again leaned heavily on Shearer in getting the win they needed to close the gap between the two sides to just one point.

At that time, there was renewed speculation about Barcelona's interest in signing him. A few weeks earlier, Newcastle chairman Sir John Hall had revealed that Barcelona had made an offer of around £20 million for the player, which had been rejected by the club. Barcelona's intention was to partner Shearer with their brilliant Brazilian striker, Ronaldo; but then, when it became clear that they would be forced to sell Ronaldo – to Inter Milan for a mind-boggling £30 million – it did not take a genius to work out that Shearer was liable to be at the very top of their shopping list of potential replacements.

Shearer took the opportunity against Poland to show that, while lacking Ronaldo's talent, he is no less influential. He put England ahead after six minutes, from a beautifully timed and weighted Paul Ince pass through the Polish defence. His potent powers of leadership from the front, his gargantuan appetite for taking on responsibility and pushing himself beyond the targets set by other players, were seen at the end of the first half. With Poland looking increasingly likely to equalise, Shearer's remarkable strength and persistence in creating a shooting chance in the most difficult circumstances inside the opponents' box led to a foul on him, and a resulting England penalty. As it turned out, Shearer uncharacteristically hit the spot-kick against a post. The example he set with his commitment to the England cause seemed to spread throughout the team, however, and the Poles started to look a demoralised side long before they were finally put out of their misery by a late Teddy Sheringham goal.

Such performances are ten a penny in the Shearer portfolio; and the more professional managers, coaches and players you talk to about him, the more you struggle to think of any football ambition which might be beyond him. Typical of their appreciation of him are the comments of Don Howe, then former England coach, and Lawrie McMenemy, who signed Shearer for Southampton as a boy and who, like Howe, was once England's assistant manager.

Among Howe's most vivid memories of Shearer is a Blackburn match at West Ham in January 1995, when the centre-forward, who had been suffering from a virus and had not been expected to play, scored a hat-trick (including two penalties) to steer his side to a 4–2 win. 'Knowing Shearer as I do, I bet he made no fuss at all about not being well before the game,' Howe said. 'I can imagine him just getting on with things and then, after the game, just mentioning in passing that he wasn't feeling well and was going home.' Howe shakes his head in wonderment and adds: 'He is a superstar, without a superstar's temperament.'

McMenemy, in charge of the England Under-21 team in which Shearer played, recalls one of the player's goals in an international match at that level against the Irish Republic in Cork. 'When he got the ball on the halfway line, just in front of where I was sitting in the dug-out, and I just shouted: "Route One", meaning that he should go forward with the ball and wait until he got into a more crowded area before releasing it. But he just kept going, and did not stop until he had crashed the ball into the net. The other lads who had been keeping up with him to make themselves available for a pass if he got into difficulties – well, they had no chance. I think that was the moment Alan revealed himself to me as a truly world-class striker.'

To McMenemy, it is possible to detect what makes Shearer so successful just by the 'cold, steely, determined look' in his eyes. Though there is unquestionably more to the player than meets your own eyes, Shearer himself – outwardly self-effacing and diplomatic to a fault – does not believe in giving any guidance. He prefers to let his boots do the talking on the field; and the only things he has revealed about himself when he is off the field, to add to the snippet that he was once nicknamed 'Smoky' because of his love of smoky-bacon-flavoured crisps, is that he likes walking the dog, playing golf and spending time with his wife Lainya and daughters, Hollie and Chloe.

In one newspaper questionnaire, the closest he came to being even mildly outrageous was when he said that the person he would most want to be stuck in a lift with was Sharon Stone, and singled out his then Blackburn team-mate Graeme Le Saux as the person he would least want to have for company in that situation (on the grounds that Le Saux had revealed Shearer's favourite record as being the less-than-cool 'Sailing' by Rod Stewart). In another questionnaire, he said that the most dangerous thing he would like to attempt is a parachute jump, but then admitted that he is scared of heights. The world figures he most admired were hostage victims Terry Waite and John McCarthy, 'for living with courage'.

Martine Delamere, in presenting an 'alternative' assessment of him, approaches it in a rather different way. The only information she is given about him is his place of birth (Newcastle upon Tyne); the date (13 August 1970) and, most importantly for the purposes of a 'personality analysis', the specific time he was delivered (4.30 p.m.). Delamere, a 38-year-old Irishwoman who uses her talents mainly in the field of counselling, then immerses herself in data, and returns with a picture of Shearer which those closest to him say is eerily accurate. It is a picture of Shearer that the public does not see; indeed, a picture that maybe in some areas the player himself might only be aware of subconsciously.

Here's what she says: 'Shearer's chart is intriguing, It is deeply puzzling in a lot of ways. The charts of most top sportsmen or sportswomen contain planets in the Fifth House, but his does not have any. So, at first glance, I would have said that this is not the chart of a professional footballer – I would have said it was maybe the chart of someone like an academic or a researcher.

'Having said that, there is one big clue from the work of a French scientist by the name of Michel Gauquelin, who once set out to disprove astrology but ended up proving to himself that there was merit in it. He made a particular study of top-class sportsmen and found that most of them had planetary activity in the Eleventh House of their charts. This relates to a person's degree of will-power and determination, and Shearer has as many as six planets in the Eleventh House, which is extraordinary. So it seems to me that his success as a footballer is down not so much to natural ability in terms of technical skills, but far more to dogged determination – an incredible ability to overcome obstacles – and the capacity for convincing himself that he is what he dreams of being. I think it is those things that have got him where he is today.

'For me, there are only two other things in his chart which would lead me to guess what he does for a living. Firstly, Sagittarius was the rising sign when he was born, which tends to make for a good physical build and a lot of mobility. Secondly, he has Jupiter, the natural ruler of Sagittarius, in the Tenth House of his chart which is basically about your public persona and ability to express yourself publicly. It is often found in the chart of a writer or an actor because Jupiter is the planet of expansion and exaggeration.

'But I believe that whatever he does for a living will always be with a view to making money, not necessarily a way in which he can express his love of the profession. I have the strong feeling that this applies to his football career. He relates money to security and vice versa. It is something that fluctuates with him, and when his financial fortunes go down, it does cause him problems of insecurity. In that way, his chart is slightly redolent of that of Terry Venables, who is also very money-motivated.

'This man is not driven by competitiveness – I don't see him as being a wildly competitive person, in the sense of wanting to beat everybody at everything he does outside football. His astrological characteristics, which make for a compulsive, obsessive person with a huge amount of physical energy, do suggest a certain degree of competitiveness. But he is in competition with himself rather than with other people. Part of his motivation is his desire to be the best player he can possibly be.

'A love of the game is not his main source of motivation either. He does have a need for adulation. He is a Leo, and Leos measure their success as human beings by the response they get from other people and always strive to do as well as they can in life. They have a liking for a high-level lifestyle, and this is particularly true of him. In his case, it is not manifested in the vulgar taste and social behaviour usually associated with people who make a tremendous amount of money without being used to it. His taste is better than that, but he is a person who will go for quality in all things. If he buys furniture for his home, for example, I think he would be the

17

type to acquire antique furniture or good reproductions – things that are liable to go up in value. To have quality in all things is what helps make him feel secure.

'Leos are also known for their loyalty. They pride themselves in "looking after" the people whom they perceive as being good to them, although I would say that Shearer can be quite judgmental and critical of people. The fact that he drives himself as hard as he does makes it difficult for him to appreciate sometimes that people are different and have different ways of doing things. He is a demanding person – I have to say that I would not particularly like to be in the position of working for him. He wouldn't make demands of anybody that he wouldn't make of himself, but the demands that he makes of himself are excessive.

'The word "workaholic" is not the sort of phrase you would normally use about a footballer, but if he were in any other occupation, that's what he would be termed. He is exceptionally one-dimensional. As snooker is the sport in which I take the most interest, the best way I can describe what I mean is to point out the difference between someone like Alex Higgins and Steve Davis. Shearer is like Davis – an automaton.

'He has a very interesting attitude to work, a very highly developed work ethic. He has a strong sense of responsibility within the workplace, and also an attitude that can create some austerity in terms of work. People with this juxtaposition of planets often work in difficult conditions or have an acceptance that work is a difficult thing and not necessarily meant to be a good form of personal expression. To people like this, work is looked upon simply as a manner in which they earn a living and they do whatever is necessary to achieve that.

'From an extremely early stage in his life, Shearer will have encountered obstacles or difficulties, maybe even health problems. Although I would say that he has two very devoted, responsible parents his chart does suggest a slightly difficult or challenging relationship with his father – a relationship in which, consciously or subconsciously, he might have felt blocked or restricted. There are signs in his chart which indicate periods of financial hardship or thriftiness during his upbringing, which might account for the importance of financial security to him. Also, if his birth time is accurate, he was born with the moon in Capricorn, and it is my experience that no matter how much attention moon-in-Capricorn people are given as kids, they tend to perceive their childhood as being lonely in some way. Often this is due to their mother going out to work and expending a lot of energy on household chores and things like that.

'I wouldn't go as far as saying he is a loner, in the sense of not wanting to be with other people, but when he needs to, he is quite capable of isolating himself and going into a world of his own. He has great stamina and endurance and in some area, either intellectually or emotionally – or just because of sheer bad luck – he will have had to tap into his sources of will-power from an early age. As a consequence, he will look upon himself as a survivor, and people who think like that inevitably always have to have something to survive.

'I have discovered this aspect in the chart of Greg Norman [the Australian golfer with a reputation for getting himself into winning positions in the major events but then failing to land the big prize]. Norman has become used to setbacks and I think his motto in life will be: "Persistence pays", or "If at first you don't succeed, try, try again". It's the same with Shearer.

'For this man, obstacles are there to be overcome – indeed, it is often when there is an obstacle to overcome that he is at his best. There is an almost perverse aspect to it with him. His attitude is: "There is a challenge there and I want to overcome it," as opposed to: "I need to overcome that challenge to get to something else." He could even be said to seek out the challenge or obstacle. When he is between a rock and a hard place, that is when his enormous resources of single-mindedness and determination truly manifest themselves.

'He would succeed in whatever he did. I mean, he is not a person who will have succeeded through luck or simply being in the right place at the right time – he will have slogged away at it and got enjoyment from that. Having said that, I should mention that he was born with Neptune in the Twelfth House of his chart – its natural home – and Neptune is the planet associated with highly developed intuition and psychic gifts. Therefore, though he would be very dismissive of such things – being the pragmatist that he is – he does have an uncanny knack of being in the right place at the right time. Generally, though, his success is all about tenacious hard slog.

'He proves the point that good motivation is often more important than real natural talent. As I have said, he will always go for the difficult target; he expects to have to work hard and have challenges to overcome; and he has this emotional need for financial security.

'Getting back for a moment to his physical qualities, it is interesting that there is so much in this chart that is cerebral. He is not by any means an unintelligent man – he has six out of the ten planets in the Ninth House, which is a sign of higher mind and intellect. This is underpinned by the position of Sagittarius, the normal ruler of the Ninth House. This alludes to tremendous optimism and a tendency to exaggerate, but it is also the sign of the eternal student, so my guess is that this man will have a very low boredom threshold; that he will always have to feel he is moving on, doing more things, learning new things. It would not surprise me at all if he were into self-development books.

'He has a great consciousness – innate maybe – that we are changing all the time, and that if we are not moving forward, we have to be moving backwards. That is something he is absolutely determined not to do, to the point where I would describe him as a "driven" man.

'Another reason for me saying this is that he has a huge amount of energy which needs to be channelled into something. So he has quite a capacity for winding himself up. This does not mean that he is an aggressive, confrontational person, but he will often be presented with a confrontational situation precipitated by someone else, and is quite capable of matching it. He is quite an assertive, intense person, and I would say that he can be quite blunt.

'Once he sets his sights on something, he is totally dedicated to it. That's partly why he might come across – publicly – as uninteresting or one-dimensional. He *is* one-dimensional in the sense that he pours so much of what he has into one area, and can only talk about what is at the centre of his life at that particular time. He is not the sort of person who could be the best footballer in the world and, at the same time, a leading expert on the works of Charlotte Brontë. He has the necessary intellectual capacity but prefers to use that side of him to further his career, and there is nothing that he will not know about the game. He is not an air-head at all – far from it; it's just that his thinking is black and white and focused on one thing.

'He is an extremely good strategist. He has three planets in Libra, which is the sign of the army general. So he will pains-takingly go to the trouble of researching the players and teams he will be up against to discover their weaknesses. He is the type who will take into account all sorts of things that other players might not even have the nous to think about – for example, the direction of the wind and the condition of the pitch. The people around him might be quite unaware that he is doing this but, believe me, he will be constantly observing and absorbing everything and adding it to his grand plan of campaign.

'Part of the reason he does this is that he has been aware from the earliest age that every stone needs to be turned over. Nothing can be left to chance. He will list the possible "screw-up" factors in everything, from washing his car to playing a major game. I think you will also find that he is a superb judge of distances and measurements. He will be one of those people who can look at a piece of furniture, say, and be able to tell you exactly what the width and length of it is without using a measuring-tape.

'Though he might come across as modest – humble even – he is supremely self-confident in certain respects. He has the capacity to sort of force himself into being whatever he wants to be, and visualises himself to be. If he absolutely believes himself to be a great footballer, then he will be. It never crosses his mind to doubt it. Though he might be unaware of the techniques of creative visualisation, that is what he employs.

'In fact, you could argue that he has a massive propensity for self-deception. I would imagine that what happens with him is that he will convince himself of something, kid himself that he can do a certain thing, and then when things happen to disabuse him of this, his stubborn streak will take over. He'll say: "But that's what I want to do. That's what I want to be," and he will work out the 30 ways he is going to do this and turn the dream into reality.

'His chart is actually well balanced in a way. Leo is the fixed sign, which relates to his tunnel vision. Such people have a loathing for change and a certain capacity for getting into terrible ruts. With Shearer, however, there is a positive manifestation of that through his single-mindedness and determination, and his good organisational ability. There are other balancing factors in his chart, which combine to make him adaptable, at least on an intellectual level. I see him as a person who will be a creature of habit in terms of his day-to-day life – the times he goes to bed, the food he eats, the clothes he wears, for example – but not in terms of his intellectuality. He is capable of making changes on that level. Once he discovers things that could improve his performance or get him where he wants to go in any area of his life, he will be happy to incorporate them into his routines. He won't change the routines, he will expand them.

'He will always try to work things out logically. Whether he always succeeds or not is a different question because he is a much more complex man than a lot of people might think, especially at the emotional end of things. But he certainly prides himself on being logical, rational and reasonable, or trying to be.

'The emotional side of things is a different kettle of fish with him. There is so much more to him than meets the eye in that respect. Deep down, he is very volatile and runs a lot of the time on nervous tension. He is highly strung – *very* highly strung, actually. There is a conflict there with regards to how he thinks he should be seen to behave. He has the moon in Capricorn, and such people are conservative with a small "c" – in his case, probably with a capital "C" as well. They are usually emotion control junkies; they will dislike any kind of public displays of emotion or affection. He likes to receive it, but he is not comfortable in expressing himself this way. It's all to do with that word "control" with him; his need to ensure that he projects the right image – how he thinks he should be seen to conduct himself – and is therefore wary of allowing people to get close enough to strip off the layers of his public self.

'His emotions are extremely complex – it is the one area in which he could be described as complicated – and I would imagine that his football career gives him an avenue through which he can direct those energies.'

My interview with Martine Delamere took place towards the end of the 1996–97 season, at a time when Shearer was out of action and his Newcastle team, in something of a transitional period following the replacement of Kevin Keegan with Kenny Dalglish as manager, were again failing to punch what their fans considered to be their full weight in the battle for major trophies. Looking ahead to the possible short-term and long-term developments in Shearer's career, Delamere said: 'There is a lot going on with him subconsciously, and a lot rising to the surface of his mind. He will be starting to question a great many things – where he is as a person and as a professional footballer – and it is a time when he will be starting the ball rolling towards major changes.

'This is a man who believes in quitting while he is ahead, so no matter how much personal success he has achieved at Newcastle, it will not have stopped him looking for new directions in his life. He is a restless person and he is now finding it increasingly easier to think unconventionally. For example, it could be that he is now ready to sacrifice financial gain for a sense of greater personal fulfilment.

'At this stage of his development, it would not surprise me if he were beginning to feel stifled and claustrophobic at Newcastle – or being in England for that matter. If it is his aim to live and play abroad then plenty of opportunities to do so are and will be presenting themselves. By nature, he is not one to act on impulse but because of the ways he is changing as a person, I can quite imagine his suddenly upping and leaving Newcastle if he were to start having disagreements and problems there. Yes, from April [1997] to December, there is a lot going on with him, a lot going on inside him.

'To my mind, he will eventually make a brilliant team manager. Being the no-half-measures person that he is, what he will be aiming for in that sphere is to manage England. That would be his big aim in life. He will be looking at Glenn Hoddle with a view to one day replacing him and, in fact, he may already be planning his strategy for doing so. He has so much to offer – the ability to work out strategies, the ability to motivate other people, good organisational and administrative skills . . . looking at his chart, I can't see how he could fail. Indeed, of all the charts I have looked at in this field [including that of Hoddle's predecessor, Terry Venables] I would say that Shearer is the man with the greatest chance of turning England into a World Cup-winning team.

'I think he would be even better as a manager than he is as a player. Playing is not his natural gift, while managing is. He would be positively Germanic in his approach. So, if he were to apply the same commitment and dedication to it, he would be just stunning.'

Unfortunately for those who have the job of countering him on the field, he would still seem to have a long way to go before stepping onto that side of the game. Despite the fears concerning the physical wear and tear to which his body has been subjected, it is possible that he will go on playing at the top level much longer than many might anticipate. Those who have worked with him feel that when he loses his effectiveness as a goalscorer, he could well add a new chapter to his career as a central-defender.

Stunning, indeed – and particularly so to the number of scouts and coaches who saw him as a schoolboy, and who had mixed feelings about the young player's chances of making it to the top . . .

CHAPTER TWO

Lost in the Crowd

The skies were grey and it was raining in Newcastle on Tuesday, 6 August 1996. But to many thousands of Newcastle United supporters, and especially to the 15,000 present at St James's Park, it was as if they were bathing in warm sunshine. The crowd, a gathering that most Football League clubs, and even one or two in the Premiership, would have been delighted to attract to any of their home matches, were not present to watch a game – they were not even in the stadium, but instead packed into the Leazes End carpark adjoining it. They were there to witness what they perceived as a golden vision of their team's future: their first glimpse of Alan Shearer as a Newcastle United player.

Upon signing for his home-town club eight days earlier, Shearer had been whisked off to the Far East to join his new team-mates on their close-season tour of Thailand, Singapore and Japan. As United themselves acknowledged with their glitzy unveiling of their mega-signing to the media and the Newcastle public on that overcast afternoon in August, the acquisition of a player of Shearer's calibre and stature and the return to the Geordie fold of one of the city's prodigal sons was worthy of a more stately welcome.

Some fans had been there for hours, during which time they were entertained by a DJ and eight scantily dressed female disco dancers. Suddenly, Alan Shearer appeared amongst them and, in an instant, the atmosphere of joy and excitement rose to the hysterical level normally reserved for a decisive Cup-final goal.

Even those whose interest in football was comparatively lukewarm found it difficult to avoid being caught up in this Shearer-mania. To outsiders, in fact, it might well have seemed perverse that, in an area with a traditionally high unemployment level, the transfer fee Newcastle paid for Shearer, not to mention his estimated £2.5 million signing-on fee and £1 million a year salary, was accepted much more than it was condemned.

Notwithstanding the business principles behind the deal from the club's point of view, the North-east has always been one of the regions of British football which, through its many years of social and economic deprivation, has best epitomised the social roots of the game in this country. Those roots are buried in the history of the game as a sport for the working class and football stadiums as theatres providing a Saturday-afternoon escape from the hardship of everyday life. No area in Britain has produced more cases of youngsters making that escape as professional footballers themselves than the North-east of England. Not for nothing was it once said that all you needed to do to find good players there was to whistle down the shaft of the nearest mine. Despite the regeneration of the North-east in recent years, following the misery experienced by the decline in old industries like shipbuilding and mining, the passion for football there has remained as strong and all-consuming as ever.

You have to be part of it to fully appreciate it, as Glenn Roeder did when the London-born defender, who had started his career at Leyton Orient and then had a long spell at Queens Park Rangers, elected to make Newcastle his next port of call in December 1983 – a period in which Alan Shearer was available to be signed by Newcastle or anybody else on schoolboy forms. Roeder, who spent more than five years at St James's Park and became club captain, recalls: 'To be quite open and honest about it, my initial thought was that I wouldn't be there that long. I had been to Newcastle on a number of occasions as a player, and all I could tell you about the place – apart from the fact that it was a bloody long way from London – was that it was a place to just get in, get a result and get home. But I soon found it was a fantastic place to be for anyone who loved football. Wherever you went, everybody wanted to know what was going on at St James's Park; for the first time in my career, I felt as if I was playing for a real football club.'

Roeder was also struck by the fact that the Geordie football passion was focused so intently on uninhibited attacking football and on great goals from great centre-forwards like Hughie Gallacher, Jackie Milburn and Malcolm Macdonald. It says much about the appeal of such figures among the Newcastle public – their need of such figures to maintain the individual 'culture' of the club – that when there was a Supporters' Club bar at St James's Park, it was named the 'No. 9 club', and that one of the conditions Shearer stipulated when negotiating his move to Newcastle was that he play in the No. 9 jersey.

'Centre-forwards are the players that the Newcastle public hang their hats on,' Roeder points out. 'Following the signing of Shearer, you can bet that most of the thousands of schoolboy players in the area who were starting to play organised football will have been calling themselves Shearer. They will all have wanted Shearer's name and number on the backs of their jerseys.'

The obvious question is why was it that Shearer, the outstanding example of the English centre-forward breed, did not get into that position at Newcastle much earlier than he did?

The young Alan was raised in a council house in Gosforth with his older sister Karen, and was encouraged to take an interest in football from an early age. When it came to birthday and Christmas presents, the options for Shearer were nothing if not clear-cut. He was only three when his father, Alan senior (who has worked for some 30 years for American Air Filters, a Cramlington-based company manufacturing industrial pollution-prevention systems), bought his son his first football. As Shearer has pointed out: 'Part and parcel of being a lad in Newcastle is that a football is thrown at your feet as soon as you can walk.'

He played superbly with it when he could run; as a schoolboy the teams who reaped the benefit of his prolific scoring included

Wallsend Boys Club and then Cramlington Juniors, the most famous of the North-east junior teams for aspiring professional footballers, as well as the Newcastle and Northumberland representative sides. The team he set his sights on playing for in the future were Newcastle United. His bedroom walls were plastered with autographed pictures of their first-team players and he himself watched virtually all of their home matches from the Gallowgate end of the ground. It was a sign of the emotive nature of that period of Shearer's life that when the newly signed player ventured onto the pitch before his Newcastle home début against Wimbledon, his first act was to symbolically boot a ball into the crowd there.

His transfer to Newcastle was packed with intriguing twists. Not the least of these was that the manager who spent so much money on him – 22 times Shearer's weight in gold, according to one publication – was Kevin Keegan; the same Kevin Keegan who, as a Newcastle striker himself, had been Shearer's boyhood idol.

At that stage in Shearer's life, Keegan, alongside similarly high-profile stars like Peter Beardsley and Chris Waddle, gave youngsters like him their biggest lift in a number of years. Newcastle were in the old Second Division when Keegan was bought for £100,000 in August 1982, and it was largely due to the player's charisma and skill that they regained their place in the top flight – following a six-year absence – in 1984. Shearer, aged 12 at the time of Keegan's arrival, queued at St James's Park for five hours to make sure he got a ticket for the great man's début against Queen's Park Rangers. In one of his videos, *Shearer on Shearer*, Keegan's position as a folk hero to him is further endorsed by the enthusiasm with which he recalls undergoing a basic skills coaching session under Keegan's guidance (the young man's prize for winning a local newspaper competition), and his experience of being one of the ball-boys for Keegan's emotional farewell game for Newcastle against Liverpool in May 1984.

Of all the Newcastle role models Shearer could have chosen, Kevin Keegan is the one who was unquestionably the most appropriate. After all, for all the honours Keegan achieved at club and international level – including his twice being voted European Footballer of the Year – the fact remained that he was a self-made great player as opposed to a natural one. Whatever talent he was blessed with was allied to an insatiable appetite for the game and for developing himself as much as it was humanly possible.

No doubt, the example Keegan set in his rise from an undistinguished start to his career with Scunthorpe was very much in Shearer's mind when the youngster, though well known to Newcastle and given a trial by the club when he had just turned 13 in August 1983, was allowed to drift away and start his professional career at the far-flung, comparatively low-key football outpost of Southampton.

In truth, the circumstances of this turn of events are not as clear-cut as some have made out. Having lost their first opportunity to sign him on schoolboy forms, Newcastle did make a strong effort to do so when Southampton, who'd had him at The Dell as a YTS apprentice professional for some two years, were deliberating on the full professional contract they could offer him. Shearer himself has subsequently helped ease Newcastle's conscience by revealing that he preferred to be at Southampton, because of the challenge of proving his sense of independence – his ability to survive so far from his family roots – and the belief that Southampton would provide a quicker route into regular first-team football for him.

In fact, when questioned on why he jumped at the first firm offer of a step into the professional game, instead of waiting a little longer for Newcastle to come to their senses, he said: 'My head ruled my heart. My instincts told me it was the right thing to do. Southampton were a smaller club than Newcastle and I knew I could develop my career out of the limelight.'

The start of his development route was different from the one Keegan had taken, in that Southampton, unlike Scunthorpe, were a First Division club. But one way in which it was the same was that Keegan, too, left home at an early age – he was born and raised not in Scunthorpe, but in Doncaster. In the context of Keegan's influence on Shearer, it might also be pertinent to point out that Keegan signed for Newcastle from – Southampton.

Still, despite all this, even Newcastle will concede that their interest in Shearer was not as hot as it could and should have been. In order to make sense of this, it is worth recalling the turmoil that the club found itself in at the time of Shearer's trial for them and the start of his link with Southampton. In 1984, immediately after Newcastle's promotion to the First Division, manager Arthur Cox sensationally ended his four-year reign at the club and joined Derby County. Such management upheavals at a club can often have a ripple effect, leading to changes throughout the whole coaching and scouting system – both personnel and method – as well as to confusion over the direction in which the club should be heading. So, to some extent, it could be argued that Newcastle were merely unlucky that Shearer came to the fore as a schoolboy at the time he did.

Perhaps the strongest mitigating factor concerns the huge number of boys a club like this can choose from, and the difficulty in assessing how each one is going to develop. Football is littered with examples of footballers who stood out as schoolboys but faded as professionals, and vice versa. Roeder recalls that two of the centre-forwards who were taken on by Newcastle as trainees during his career with the club were Shearer's fellow Wallsend Boys Club stars, David Robinson and Tony Lormor. Both played with Shearer (who, because of his August birthday, was eligible under the regulations of junior football to appear in two age-group teams) and both were similarly prolific scorers. But the pair made only a handful of first-team appearances for Newcastle and have since drifted into the comparative anonymity of the lower divisions, although Lormor did reappear in the national spotlight in the 1996–97 season as a member of the Chesterfield squad in the FA Cup semi-final.

In Shearer's case, almost all the coaches and scouts who watched him when he was in his teens point out that although his scoring record in schoolboy football was impressive, a close inspection of his basic ability revealed not a great deal more than reasonable pace (as opposed to explosive quickness), a good right foot and a positive attitude.

Some players stand out as 'born' footballers. For example, you did not need to be an expert on the finer points of football to recognise that Paul Gascoigne – who was born and bred in Gateshead, joined Newcastle from school and first made his mark in Newcastle's team after their 1984 promotion-winning success – was a special player, at least in the technical sense. Plump and undisciplined he might have been, but from a very early age the tricks he could perform with a ball took the breath away. It was different with Shearer; because of the 'quality' of the youngsters available to Newcastle at that time, he was viewed as a borderline case.

Glenn Roeder, an articulate, perceptive professional who went on to become a manager at Gillingham and then Watford, and who has recently been deployed as a scout and coach in Glenn Hoddle's England set-up, has mixed views on the subject: 'The first thing you look for in any young player is his skill on the ball. Can he control the ball first time? What does he do on it? Can he read the game? Thereafter, you start looking at him in a bit more depth, and assess his attitude, dedication and work-rate, things like that.' However, if anyone can talk with authority on how you can be too dazzled by that skill-factor, it is Roeder. He was the Newcastle player who became closest to the outrageously gifted but notoriously self-destructive Gascoigne; so much so that when Gazza moved to Lazio, Roeder, a counsellor and confidant to the player at Newcastle, was chosen to join him there to help him to get into the groove of adopting the right professional habits. But Roeder found it such a strain that he and his family returned to England six months later.

All this, together with the 'mistake' Newcastle made with Shearer, leads Roeder to the view that English football would do well to look at the scouting philosophy of top Dutch club Ajax. He explains: 'Somewhere in that club, there is a sign which says

"TIPS". Each letter stands for a specific aspect of the game – T for technique, or ball skills; I for football intelligence; P for personality, i.e. attitude; S for speed – and it represents the club's list of individual coaching priorities. When the scouts are looking at potential young Ajax players, however, they have to imagine the sign being turned upside down to read: "SPIT". Technical ability is at the bottom of the list of priorities because it is something that, to a great extent, can be taught or improved. You could argue that this is true of most things, but they feel that speed is more of a God-given asset – which I agree with – and on the managerial experience I have had, I can certainly vouch for the fact that it is the same with attitude.

'Shearer is not particularly quick, but he is not particularly slow either – not when he gets into his stride. I would say he is a strong runner, so he would probably have got into Ajax on that basis, and he would definitely have got into Ajax on his attitude.'

But would it have occurred to Ajax that they might have a £15 million player on their hands? It certainly did not occur to the men who watched him during his schoolboy career; and, though they recognise that they dropped a clanger in not being more conscious of the significance of what he had to offer, they insist that given the same set of circumstances, they would probably adopt the same stance again.

When Shearer did eventually sign for Newcastle, the media clamour for information about his background as a youngster in the North-east brought forth views and recollections about him from what seemed to be a cast of hundreds. Most of these views came from the men who had rubbed shoulders with Shearer as team-mates but who had never had the chance to earn a living from the game. From one of these – in *The Sun* – we learned that Shearer was nicknamed 'Chinky' because 'his eyes screwed right up when he smiled', and that he also attracted much good-natured stick because his hair fringe 'stuck flat against his forehead like he was wearing a Roman helmet'.

Gary Hayes, one of his boyhood friends, and someone who at

least managed to gain a foothold in the professional game at non-league level, recalled his street 'matches' with Shearer. 'We'd play across the road, one-against-one, with the kerbstones as goals. It was 10p a goal and I lost nearly all the time. Sometimes I would lose £2, all my pocket money.' Equally revealing about Shearer's competitive instincts was the anecdote from a Wallsend Boys Club coach, Les Howie, about one of the few matches in which Shearer – usually good for 50 goals a season for them – was struggling to find his finishing touch. According to Howie, Shearer's father suddenly shouted: 'Bet you a quid you can't score!' and the young Alan immediately responded to the challenge with three goals in five minutes.

Of all the people associated with Shearer in those days, however, Peter Kirkley, Brian Clark and Jimmy Nelson can present a particularly clear picture of his qualities. Kirkley and Clark were closely involved with the Wallsend BC teams in which he played from the age of nine to 15. Jimmy Nelson was the coach of his Gosforth High School team and also the manager of Shearer's Northumberland Boys XI.

One thing these three men have in common is that between the time Shearer had his Newcastle United trial and was snapped up by Southampton – a period of some 11 months – they were all involved in Newcastle's schoolboy scouting and coaching set-up, too. Kirkley, a Newcastle scout, became their full-time youth development officer. Clark was (and still is) a prominent Newcastle scout, and Nelson was (and still is) a member of Newcastle's part-time schoolboy coaching staff.

Nelson, once a full-back on the books of Sunderland and Ipswich, had been the first member of the trio to be alerted to Shearer's scoring ability, mainly because of the fact that Gosforth High School (for pupils between the age of 13 and 16) shared the same grounds as the first school Shearer attended – Grange First School – from the age of five to nine. Grange's caretaker, a man by the name of Norman Teasdale, also happened to be responsible for the cleaning at Gosforth High, and Nelson recalls: 'He marked my card about Alan some five years before I became associated with him. Grange was a typical first school, in that almost all the teachers were women, so Norman, being a keen footballer and football fan, used to help the headmaster in running the school team. It was only six- or seven-a-side stuff, but all the mums and dads would be there, and it was always a nice occasion. Alan would have been six or seven when he started playing for the team, and even then I remember Norman being more enthusiastic about him than anyone. He actually said to me: "Jim, if you are still there in a few years' time in charge of the High School team, I have a great player coming through to you."

'I liked to have the side for the full three years that the boys were there, so I would take the lads from the age of 13 – in the Under-14 side – through to 16, then start again. As luck would have it, I was in charge of the 13-year-olds when Alan joined the school [from Gosforth Middle School], so I had him straightaway.'

Nelson is lavish in his praise of Shearer, both as a pupil and as a person. 'The thing about Alan was that he always gave his best,' Nelson says. 'He never complained – he just got on with it. We occasionally use Alan as an example in school assemblies but we hardly ever mention football. We talk about how he behaved in class, and how we would expect him to behave in certain situations. For example, we have quite a high Asian population in the school and a year or two ago there were a couple of incidents of bullying which turned into quite a big racial issue. So the deputy headmaster and I organised an assembly on how we thought Alan Shearer would have reacted had he been in their position. We were not preaching that people should always turn the other cheek, but we felt it pertinent to point out the number of times Alan gets kicked and does not retaliate.

'We [the school] have actually organised an Alan Shearer Sports Award and it will not be just for sporting excellence but also how the pupil has behaved. I don't know Alan's parents, but judging from the way he conducted himself at school, I would say that he had an extremely good upbringing. One of the great things about him was that he never bragged. If you were to ask him what he liked doing, he would just say: "I like playing football" and leave it at that. You would never hear him talking about how good he was, the number of goals he scored, the teams he played for, the clubs that were showing an interest in him. This was one of the reasons why every member of staff liked him.

'He has not changed. I can walk into the Newcastle United players' lounge now, and he'll come straight across to have a chat, and make a great fuss of my lad, James. It's nice.

'It was his character that initially endeared him to me. One of the school teams in which he played wasn't a very good side and, to make sure that he wasn't starved of the ball, we used him mainly in midfield. He was by far our best player. You know those long, surging runs of his, where he will pick the ball up in a deep position, surge forward with it, going past maybe two or three opponents and finish with an explosive shot into the net? Well, he was doing that quite often for us. But he never boasted about it; and though he was having to do so much of the work in helping us win matches, he never complained about his lot or slaughtered the players in his team who were not as good as him.

'The thing with him was not whether his team-mates were good enough, but that they gave their all. As I said, Alan tried as hard as he could. Football was the thing he loved and most of his energies went into that. Although he wasn't academically minded enough to be in the top six as far as his schoolwork was concerned, he wasn't in the bottom six either. With most subjects, if not all, you could say that he was Mr Average really. But he did try and he was no trouble to anybody.

'People sometimes ask me what I think he would have done for a living had he not been a professional footballer. It's hard to say. He himself always said: "I want to be a professional footballer" and obviously something inside him told him he could be. A lot of kids say that, and as a teacher you are inclined to take it with a pinch of salt. Saying it is one thing, but doing it is another, you know? A lot of kids focus on it just to avoid the pressures of having to do well in their schoolwork and getting the right job.

'Alan actually made it clear in his careers interview that he wanted to be a professional footballer. The careers people came back to me to ask what chance he had and, of course, with Alan having become attached to Southampton, it was obvious he had a chance. So that was the end of any desire we might have had to steer him into something else. Actually, when Alan was signed by Newcastle, the media made out that he had been given careers advice not to try and be a footballer, which is totally untrue. All that happened was that our deputy headmaster, who happens to be a football fanatic, said to Alan: "There are many more players who don't make the grade than those who do, so just stick at your schoolwork and exams in case you don't make it."'

Interestingly, the message was put across even more forcibly by Shearer's father, a man noted among those who know him for preaching the importance of keeping your feet on the ground. Alan senior has admitted that it was only when his son was signed by Southampton as an associate schoolboy that he began to feel confident of his chances of earning a living from the game; and, even then, he never tired of reminding his son not to take anything for granted. Indeed, during Shearer's schoolboy career, there were times when Alan senior came across as being as negative as Shearer was positive.

In an interview with the Southampton *Evening Echo*, at the time of Shearer's scoring England début against France at Wembley in March 1993, Alan senior revealed: 'I kept telling him it was a very hard profession to get into, but he was always adamant that this was what he was going to do. No one and nothing was going to stop him. I always thought he could do it if he got a chance, but I knew it was going to be difficult and I was just trying to prepare him in case it did not happen. I just wanted him to be realistic and acknowledge the possibility that he might have to come back and work in a factory. But he refused even to consider the possibility of failure.'

Failure? Although the only academic qualification under

Shearer's belt when he left school at 16 was a GCSE in English, Jimmy Nelson insists: 'The one thing I am sure about with Alan is that whatever he would have done for a living, he would not have struggled. He did once take part in a vocational initiative aimed at giving pupils an insight into various careers. He opted for information technology, which involved a lot of basic computer word-processing, graphic and programming work, and I understand that he handled it as well as anybody. To me, he would not have gone into a manual job – it would have been something that required a bit of nous. I have the feeling that he would have made an ideal old-fashioned apprentice in a field such as engineering or draughtsmanship, something like that. It would have been something sensible, practical.'

But scoring goals was what Shearer did best, and Nelson's admiration for that ability was endorsed by all the other people who were to come into contact with the striker as he grew older and ever more prolific.

It was shortly after Nelson's initial link with Shearer that Peter Kirkley and Brian Clark came into the picture, and brought him to Wallsend BC. Kirkley, who ran the boys' club for a number of years – during which time the club produced players such as Peter Beardsley and Steve Bruce and, more recently, Newcastle first-teamers Steve Watson, Robbie Elliott and Lee Clark – also had a full-time job as assistant manager of Wallsend Sports Centre and was Burnley's North-east scout.

Clark worked with him, coaching one of the Wallsend BC's teams (of which there were eight, ranging from Under-10 to Under-16) and helping Kirkley ensure that Burnley did not miss anyone with the potential to be of use to them.

Clark, who was later to work with Kirkley at Newcastle (and gain the distinction of bringing Gascoigne to the club) knew Shearer's father. He went to the same school as Alan senior in the east-end Newcastle suburb of Walker, and happened to come across him – for the first time since boyhood – when Shearer was playing for Gosforth Middle School.

Clark recalls: 'It was an Under-11 game and I was just there because I'd been tipped off about a player in the same team. So Alan senior was there, and he came across to say hello. He's a very nice lad, like Alan; they're a nice family – I really mean that. Anyway, he said: "What are you doing here – you got a son playing?" I said no, and asked if he had. "Aye," he said. "That's my lad over there." I started watching Alan for a while, and I'm thinking: "Oh aye, he's a good player." That's how he came to Wallsend.

'The thing I remember the most about him was his confidence. He was very, very sure of himself – quiet but sure, you know what I mean? If he had something to say, he would say it. He would keep questioning things, and I used to say: "That lad shouldn't be questioning us." But he didn't do it in a disrespectful way. Quiet but sure; yes, that was him.'

Wallsend were fortunate. Such clubs, forming a bewildering myriad of leagues for youngsters to act out their soccer fantasies, cannot play boys living outside a five-mile radius, and Shearer only just qualified. He went on to help Wallsend win numerous trophies in his six years there, before switching camps and spending a season with Cramlington Juniors, their arch rivals, at the age of 15.

It has been claimed that his move, which was tantamount to someone leaving Liverpool to join Manchester United, and which was to rebound on Wallsend's Under-16 team more heavily than the club's officials had anticipated, stemmed partly from Shearer's friendship with Gary Hayes, a Cramlington player. It has also been suggested that it might have had something to do with the fact that Kirkley, more influential at Newcastle than any of the other figures associated with Shearer then, appeared indifferent to the club's lukewarm interest in the player. This could not have endeared Kirkley to Shearer and his family, although Cramlington's chairman then, Jimmy Snowdon, prefers to attribute Shearer's departure to Wallsend's squad system ('They liked to keep changing their team and there were matches where Alan was on the sidelines') and his powers of persuasion.

'This is going to sound really terrible, but I think Alan signed for Cramlington because of me,' says Snowdon. 'In fact, he says it himself. When I ask him why he came to Cramlington, he says that it was because I talked him into it. When I rang Alan's dad up to ask if Alan would be interested in joining us, his first reaction was: "Well, Alan's quite happy at Wallsend." However, he had a quick word with Alan, and said that I could pop around for ten minutes to have a chat about it. As it turned out, I was sat there for two hours. I sold Cramlington to Alan not just on the basis of our having a good Under-16 team, but also on our being a fun club. You know, although we took our football seriously, we believed in players being able to have a laugh and a joke in training, and we would do strange things like take them for a walk on the beach or for a meal in a hotel before big matches. Our approach was a little bit different from that of a lot of other clubs. I think Alan was attracted to us partly because I made him laugh, to be honest.'

It was no laughing matter to Wallsend. That season Shearer scored some 50 goals; and his Cramlington Under-16 team became the youngest side to win the Northumberland FA Junior Cup, a competition for Under-18 sides. Shearer's refusal to be overawed by any occasion, which had made him a key player for the Northumberland Boys Under-19 county team when he was only 15, was again shown in the FA Junior Cup final when he scored the only goal from a last-minute penalty.

So Cramlington's gain was very much Wallsend's loss, although Peter Kirkley likes to think that Shearer had good cause to be grateful for his experiences at Wallsend. 'If you ask any of the boys we have had what they learned at the club, I think they would say discipline,' he explains. 'It came from the top – I never appointed a manager or coach without vetting him. It had to be the right person. The players had to abide by certain rules concerning things like what to wear, how we expected them to conduct themselves both on and off the pitch – really, our aim was not just to produce good footballers but also good citizens. Some clubs had one or two nutters; their attitude was: "If they can play, they can play." But ours was that the image of Wallsend BC always had to come first. If you weren't prepared to abide by our rules, you went.'

Shearer was tailor-made for Wallsend Kirkley recalls: 'He was a great lad to deal with. He was quite boisterous, but he wasn't a hooligan, far from it. He never did anything that might get him into bother. We trained one night a week and played on the Sunday, and although Alan lived further from the club than the rest, he was never late; he was always there when you wanted him to be there. This applied to other things. If anything was organised – even table-tennis and other things outside football – he would always be there taking part.'

It was not difficult for Kirkley to warm to Shearer as a goalscorer, too. 'He scored so many of his goals by breaking through from deep positions,' he says. 'Although he was slightly built he had the wonderful knack of being able to hold off opponents. He would gain half a yard on an opponent, then get his body between the opponent and switch the ball to the foot furthest away from the other player. He made it so difficult for people to get in tackles on him. I think he is a great example to any youngster coming into the game.'

This leads Kirkley back to that word 'attitude', in this particular instance Shearer's determination not to allow the setback of his perceived rejection by Newcastle to undermine his confidence. As for the part he played in that rejection, Kirkley stresses that he was not officially Newcastle's youth development officer when Shearer had his trial there; that he was still technically employed by Wallsend Sports Centre. He had been offered the Newcastle youth development officer job by United's manager Arthur Cox, following the tragic death of the previous incumbent, Brian Watson, but after accepting it, he experienced some difficulty in getting released from his existing post as quickly as he and Newcastle would have wished. To his credit, however, Kirkley does not offer this as an excuse. In fact, he admits that even when it became possible for him to have a bigger influence in the matter, he elected not to do so.

41

Explanations of what exactly happened to the striker at Newcastle tend to be vague and contradictory. For example, although it is a fact that Shearer was deployed by Newcastle as a goalkeeper, much to the club's embarrassment when this was revealed at the time of their multi-million-pound acquisition of him, it was a situation of his own making.

Shearer himself has suggested that he might have tried to do too much. 'I thought I could do everything,' he said. 'I thought very highly of myself. I thought I could score from corners, goal-kicks – I was just one of those kids who wanted to do everything.'

Kirkley says: 'You could say that Alan just got lost in the crowd. What the club used to do at holiday times was herd as many young-sters in as possible. They would have had maybe 70 or 80 kids there, so all the coaches used to do was organise matches amongst them. As it happened, they were short of goalkeepers, so when they said: "Anybody fancy playing in goal?" Alan put his hand up. This would have been typical of him because he was always willing to help people out – he was that type of lad. Also, you have to remember that it was quite natural for him to want to have a go in that position because he always liked to go in goal in the boys club kickabouts. He did it in matches, too – if we were winning comfortably, say 6–0 or 7–0, and he had scored the bulk of them, he would go between the sticks to give the keeper a chance to get into the game. I think Alan spent a big part of his trial period in goal, if not all of it, and that was it.'

Jimmy Nelson, one of the trialists' coaches, says: 'He didn't play in goal all the time. He was there from Monday to Friday, and the time was broken up with playing matches – eight-a-side games across the pitch – training, working and just getting a look at things. Yes, Alan did play in goal, but only as part of one of the afternoon sessions.

'It's not that Newcastle did not fancy Alan as a player, far from it,' Nelson continues. 'But if memory serves me right, that group of trialists also included players like Tommy Johnson and Paul Kitson [now with Celtic and West Ham respectively] . . . it was a good vintage crop of lads on trial at Newcastle that week. With hindsight, I think that perhaps we just took too long to make up our minds about Alan. It was a case of: "We'll see you again during your next holiday." By then, of course, he'd gone to Southampton.'

As with Kirkley, the obvious question is whether Nelson, who knew more than most about Shearer through his school association with him, could – and should – have done more to use his position at St James's Park to force Newcastle to take notice of him. But Nelson says: 'When I joined Newcastle, I was told I had to be totally impartial; that I was just a coach and on no account could I attempt to recruit someone for the club, outside of maybe recommending him. That, in fact, is still the case today. Very few schoolteachers work for professional clubs and while you might want to say to the manager or chief scout: "Hey, come down to my school and have a look at this lad," you can be treading on very dangerous ground if you try to do more than that. This was certainly the case when I started at Newcastle and, to be honest, even now I would have to be very careful about things like this.'

Nelson is not sure how strongly he would have been prepared to recommend Shearer to Newcastle anyway. Referring again to the standard of many of his contemporaries, he makes the point that although Shearer did attract the attention of a handful of league clubs as a schoolboy – in addition to Newcastle and Southampton, both Manchester City and Derby were also known to be keeping tabs on him – the general attitude to the prospect of signing him hardly evoked visions of scouts being injured in a rush. 'Alan always struck me as being a very good player, but if anyone had said to me then that he was going to be one of the best strikers in Europe, I would have had to disagree,' Nelson says.

'Of all the junior players I have worked with, the best was probably Trevor Steven [who was a member of his Northumberland County side and who was taken to Burnley by Kirkley]. One of the coaches I worked with, Tommy Cavanagh, used to say: "There is only one thing that's going to stop Trevor becoming a leading professional player and that's a bus." You couldn't really say that about Alan. I thought he would have a career in the game, but I never thought that he would reach the heights that Trevor did.'

Nelson even goes as far as to suggest that starting his career at Southampton might have been more beneficial to Shearer than doing so with Newcastle. 'One of the hardest things for players in that situation is coping with living away from home. Don't get me wrong – there was nothing wrong with Alan's home life, far from it, but I have the feeling that being so far from home stood him in good stead. He was always a very mature lad, but this probably added a different dimension to his character.'

The teacher certainly gets full marks for his honesty – as do Kirkley and Clark. The latter, who could never be accused of having undergone a passion bypass operation when it comes to warming to genuine footballing talent, and especially talent in the black-and-white striped shirt of his beloved Newcastle United, had no qualms about going out on a limb on Gascoigne.

Clark had first set eyes on Gazza in a match in which he had been asked by Newcastle to watch someone else. 'My eyes were immediately drawn to this little fat lad – and when I say fat, I mean fat,' Clark recalls. 'But you couldn't fail to be impressed by his skill on the ball. His mates on the touchline were loving it – they were calling him "Bamber" [a nickname coined from the boffin-like Bamber Gascoigne, the original quiz-master of the *University Challenge* TV programme] – and he was playing to them. You know, winking and smiling and being daft. He didn't have much pace, but he had strength, and his passing – well, no matter what the distance, he hit the target every time.'

Clark, though, had some difficulty in persuading his boss at St James's Park, Brian Watson, that the England-star-to-be had rather more going for him than the player the scout had been assigned to study. 'Oh, Gascoigne is crap,' Watson told him. Clark disagreed and, over the ensuing weeks, his backing of Gazza became almost a personal crusade. Watson's disagreement, on the grounds of Gascoigne's unathletic build and his self-indulgent ball tricks, led to so much friction between him and Clark that, on one occasion, the pair virtually came to blows over the issue. Clark was immediately sacked by Watson, then reinstated sufficiently quickly for him to get Gascoigne signed for Newcastle just before Middlesbrough – also hot on his trail – could sign him.

Did Shearer provoke such strong emotions in him? Clark shrugs, and recalls Shearer's schoolboy move from Wallsend to Cramlington. 'Normally, if Peter Kirkley lost a good player, he would go running after him, and try and get him back. But that didn't happen with Alan Shearer – we just let him go. This might sound stupid now, me being a scout, but never in my wildest dreams did I think Alan would be a £15 million player. A good player, definitely, but for me there was never that shining light you get when you watch a brilliant player. Honestly, I can't say he was brilliant at that age, because he wasn't. I would be telling lies if I said any different.'

Kirkley nods in agreement. 'I am delighted for Alan that he has done so well, but I have to put my hand on my heart and say that, given all the circumstances, I still think I did the right thing. Compared with other strikers Newcastle were interested in, I felt he was a bit too slow. He still runs like he used to, doesn't he? He still has the long stride that he had at nine. He has got a change of pace, a surge, but it isn't dramatic. In fact, we used to describe him as being a bit one-paced, you know? He was also quite slight and I think the strength he showed came not from his physique but from the fact that he had a big heart.'

Fortunately for Shearer, at least one of the men in a position to put him on the first rung of the professional football ladder deemed that big heart a much more significant factor than others.

CHAPTER THREE

Hixon's Steal

Jack Hixon is a 77-year-old former British Rail white-collar employee living in the Northumberland seaside resort of Whitley Bay. He is a spritely, genial figure who oozes down-to-earth Geordie charm, common sense and honesty – the sort of man people find it easy to confide in and trust.

Alan Shearer does. So much so that hardly a day goes by without him talking to Hixon. No matter where he might be in the world, or how heavy his commitments, it would be unthinkable for Shearer not to create the time to give Hixon a call.

The reason for this is that Shearer, unlike a number of other people who have emerged from humble beginnings to find fame and fortune, is not the type to forget those who gave him a helping hand on the way; and as Hixon is the man who 'discovered' him when he was 13, and was responsible for bringing him to Southampton, Shearer inevitably feels a closer affinity with him than anyone else.

Hixon is not the only figure from Shearer's past who has not been overlooked throughout the footballer's rise to fame and fortune. Another who can be said to have a special place in his wide circle of friends and acquaintances is his former Cramlington Boys Club mentor, Jimmy Snowdon. When Shearer played for the club between the ages of 15 and 16, Snowdon treated him more like one of his children than one of his players. On matchdays it was not unusual for Shearer to go to Snowdon's house hours before kick-off for tea and biscuits and a chat with his son and daughter. The player still keeps in touch with Snowdon and his family to this day.

'We became friends, and we still are friends,' Snowdon says. 'From time to time, we'll go out for a beer together and, in some ways, our relationship is really little different from the one we had when he was playing for me. He's a good guy, a very sincere young man. There's no way you could dish any dirt on him even if you wanted to, because there just isn't any. There are no airs and graces with him.'

It was typical of Shearer that when he was invited to the stag party of his England team-mate David Platt – a day at Ascot races – he telephoned Snowdon for advice on which horses to back. 'I know nothing about horseracing,' he said. 'Can you select a horse for me in each race?' Equally characteristic was his willingness to accede to Snowdon's request to open the new Cramlington club-house and to sign what seemed an endless number of autographs at the event. 'The place was mobbed,' Snowdon recalls, 'and the patience Alan showed was remarkable. Not one person who asked for his autograph was turned down – he made himself available to everybody. We had a pint together the other week,' Snowdon adds, 'and Alan was telling me that during his recovery from a groin injury, he actually had autograph requests from two women while he was sitting in the sauna of his local health club. The ladies, fully clothed I should add, had no compunction about just knocking on the door and asking him. That gives you an idea of how the public here look upon him – as I said, he is an ordinary guy and is the same now as he was when he was a lad.

'His parents are exactly the same. His mother still goes to work – in the Social Services – as does his dad. I said to Alan senior: "Why don't you retire?" and he replied: "What would I do with my time Jimmy? I'm learning to play golf, but that wouldn't be enough to keep myself occupied. Besides anything else, all my mates are at work." It's a horrible cliché but Alan's parents are ordinary working people, the same as me, and they don't try to pretend they are any different. This is one of the things I think Alan has inherited from them, and it's why he has attracted so much respect.'

Not surprisingly for someone so close to Shearer, Snowdon has a great affection for Jack Hixon, too. He has known Hixon – the 'scouting doyen', as he calls him – for some 20 years, which gives him the licence to wind the other man up as well as praise him. 'What a man,' he says, tongue-in-cheek. 'We were invited to Alan's wedding [at Southampton] and I drove Jack down. Nightmare – I had to listen to all his war stories. At the end of the journey, even the car was in a bad way, never mind me.'

Shearer has been subjected to these stories even more, because Hixon has become not just a friend, but his honorary grandfather. 'When Alan says in the media that he owes everything to me,' Hixon jokes, 'I feel like saying: "Well, why don't you pay me then?" But behind the wisecracks, it is clearly a highly emotional subject for him.

Lawrie McMenemy, the Southampton manager who brought Hixon to the club as a scout, recalls how moved the older man was when Shearer picked up his first Footballer of the Year award in 1994, from the Football Writers' Association. Shearer insisted on bringing Hixon down to London to be with him at the awards dinner at the Royal Lancaster Hotel and McMenemy says that 'the tears were tumbling off Jack's cheeks' as he listened to the speeches praising him for unearthing such a precious jewel of a player.

Though Shearer is more pragmatic about it, at least publicly, his feelings for Hixon also run deep. Hixon says: 'People say: "He's in his 20s and you're in your 70s – there's a bit of an age gap there. Where do you find common ground?" Well, the other fellow can be in his 70s mentally. He's an amazing fellow – worldly-wise in the best sense of the word.

'Wherever he goes – even when he goes to places like Moldova – my phone will ring, and there will be that deep voice on the other end of the line asking: "Ho Hixon – any news?" He was in Finland [in an England training camp in preparation for the 1992 European Championship finals in Sweden] and he was supposed to be incommunicado, but I still got my call. I think he looks upon it as a bit of a challenge.'

In every match in which Shearer plays, Hixon places a bet on him scoring the first goal. Thus, when Shearer telephones Hixon on the eve of a match, he will usually sign off by saying: 'I'll be in touch tomorrow to tell you about my goals.' It became so much of a ritual when he was at Blackburn that his fellow striker, Mike Newell, telephoned Hixon himself and mimicked his colleague saying: 'Ho Hixon, I've rung to talk about my goals.'

Shearer, too, is not averse to having some fun with the old man, feigning disgust if Hixon has not been there to take his call ('That's it, Hixon – you've had it'), and gently attempting to provoke him into doing or saying something out of character. Hixon, who feels obliged to send Shearer a good-luck card before every England match ('I think he would be almost offended if he didn't get one'), says: 'Sometimes Alan rings from the car, and you've got to be careful what you say because he can have the speaker on, and you never know who he has with him. You know, he can lead you into things sometimes.'

Perhaps typical of the rapport between the two was their conversation when Shearer made contact with Hixon from his new Jaguar while he was driving back to Blackburn after taking delivery of the vehicle in Coventry. The pair, in blokeish mood, teased each other about 'playing' with a 'rubber duck' in the bath. Referring to the goals Shearer had scored the previous weekend, Hixon then told him: 'I'll tell you what, you probably get more kisses and cuddles from your centre-half than you do from your missus.'

'Oh no he doesn't,' exclaimed an indignant female voice.

'Is that Lainya with you?' Hixon asked.

'Aye,' Shearer replied, laughing – affectionately – at the old man's embarrassment.

Shearer's sense of responsibility towards Hixon, his willingness to bring him into his world and share his best moments with him, was again highlighted when he rang him on his journey home from Newcastle's stunning 5–0 home win over their arch rivals,

Manchester United, last season. 'What about that?' Shearer said.

'Oh great,' Hixon replied. 'I'm so delighted for you. But why couldn't you have got the first goal? I got 4 to 1 on it, and what do you do? You get the fourth. How can I bet on that?'

Shearer giggled. 'We stuffed them.'

'I know,' Hixon said. 'You did great.'

'Aye, we stuffed them,' Shearer continued, milking Hixon's verbal applause.

At that point, the player told him that Simon Marsh, the promotions manager of Umbro (the sportswear company endorsed by Shearer) was in the car. Umbro's kit is used by Manchester United and Marsh is a United supporter. So Shearer took delight in passing him onto Hixon who, by now, was as highly charged as the player. 'Oh, you've ditched your bloody red shirt, have you?' Hixon asked.

Hixon has the same rapport with Shearer's parents. Each Friday afternoon, when Alan senior finishes work at lunchtime, he and Hixon meet for a drink at a working-men's club. More often than not, they are joined by the father of Tommy Widdrington (a midfielder who was also pushed in Southampton's direction by Hixon and who is now with Grimsby); the father of the Newcastle defender, Steve Watson; Paddy Lowrie, the assistant manager of Hixon's local club, Whitley Bay; and Jackie Marks, a former coach to another non-league club, Blyth Spartans. 'We can be anything up to 12-handed and the only subject of conversation is football,' Hixon says. 'Alan's parents are absolutely superb, so homely and down-to-earth. Alan senior won't be interviewed by the media, did you know that? He has so much pride in Alan, it's bursting out of him. But he never portrays that proud-parent image of saying: "Our kid did this" or "Our kid did that". It's not his scene.'

Hixon, however, more than makes up for it. Quite apart from Shearer's ability as a footballer, he waxes lyrical on the 'presence' of Shearer, in the context of the manner in which his fellow England players relate to him as their leader off the pitch as well as on it, and on Shearer's 'immense natural dignity'. He explains: 'Some people say he's dull because he doesn't get into controversial areas, but that does not mean he doesn't express his feelings.' Indeed, to those closest to him, Shearer has revealed that, in common with other strikers who focus so much of their energies on getting the ball into the net, the experience of scoring a goal can be more exciting to him than sex. Hixon's point is that Shearer's sense of propriety is unusually high, and always has been. 'I have known that boy since he was 13 – no, I should correct that by saying I have known that man since he was 13 – and although he uses the same foul language as other players at times, you never hear him use swear words as part of his conversational flow. As a matter of fact, he never swears in front of me. He doesn't do it in front of his family, and he has always said that he looks upon me as being part of it. People say it's a measure of his respect for me, but I think it is a sign of the respect he has for himself.

'He engenders respect,' Hixon adds. 'He leads by example. I know that this is one of the maxims that everybody trots out, but he fulfils all the criteria you see.'

Hixon, who like Shearer was born and raised on Tyneside and was a Newcastle fan as a boy, was no more than a run-of-the-mill schoolboy player. 'I only played at school, at right-back,' he recalls. 'If I had been a scout watching me, I would have been bloody disgusted.' His only claim to fame as an adult player was that when he was in the United States during his National Service in the Navy, he took part in a match against the Harvard All-Stars.

'But in trying to justify myself,' he argues, 'let me just say that George Whiting [the late sports writer on the London *Evening Standard*] was probably the foremost boxing correspondent of all time, but I would not have liked to see him in the ring with Chris Eubank.' Indeed, as a judge of footballers in the context of the role of league club talent-spotter, Hixon, who is now carrying out that function in the North-east on Ipswich's behalf, is among the most respected men in the business.

The opportunity to initially break into this side of the game came in 1950 when Billy Elliott, one of the game's leading wingers and a Hixon shipmate in the Navy, joined Burnley and asked him to inform the club of any good prospects he came across in the North-east. Hixon did this for 17 years – ten of which were spent as chief scout – and during this time a total of 27 players recommended to the club by him went on to become first-team players. These included John Angus, Ralph Coates, Ray Pointer and Dave Thomas, all of whom became England internationals.

Hixon left Burnley at a time when the long managerial reign of Harry Potts was coming to an end and the club were grooming Jimmy Adamson, their former captain and then the first-team coach, to take over from him. Hixon is reticent about discussing publicly how this affected him, but as a man who sets a great store by relationships, it was perhaps inevitable that he should perceive the curtain being drawn on Potts as a sign that it might also be time for him to fade out of the Turf Moor picture. It is also worth noting that Hixon is an immensely proud man, and that Adamson, in eulogising over the standard of the Burnley coaching staff, might well have put his foot in it when he talked about the club's ability to produce first-class players from 'second-class' raw material.

Hixon then had brief spells attached to Derby, Stoke City and Blackpool ('I was wandering in the wilderness looking for a chosen tribe'), before being head-hunted by Lawrie McMenemy for Southampton in January 1974.

If anybody was desperate to get access to the rich seam of football talent in the North-east it was McMenemy, who had cut his managerial-coaching teeth at Gateshead, his home-town club, and Bishop Auckland, and who appreciated that the future for any small-town club could only be as impressive as its schoolboy system. Appreciating the logistical difficulty in repeatedly bringing North-east schoolboys down to Hampshire for trials, McMenemy hired Gateshead Stadium for the purpose. 'We established our own schoolboy centre of excellence in the area,' he recalls. 'I am not sure it was called that in those days, but I think we were one of the first clubs in the league – if not the first – to establish training centres in other areas where youngsters could get qualified coaching from us without having to travel to Southampton. We would eventually bring them down in their school holidays and assess them by integrating them with the trainee professionals, or apprentices as they were called then, in matches.

'Jack was the head of a three-man scouting team and, although he was not the only person involved in the set-up – at one time, we had Jim Montgomery [the former Sunderland goalkeeper] helping with the coaching, for example – it was very much his little empire. He did a tremendous job for us. People involved in schoolboy football in the North-east have so much respect and warmth for him, you see. Also, he's a wily bird and he really put himself about for us. It wasn't just a question of his watching matches. He'd spend a lot of time socialising with the boys' parents and things like that. He was exceptionally thorough. He didn't miss a trick.'

The first North-east players Hixon and his colleagues pushed Southampton's way were George Shipley and Tony Sealey, who went on to become first-team players before being sold to other clubs. But although not all the players that Hixon and his counterparts in other areas brought to the club could be said to have set the place alight, the transfer fees Southampton received for them helped finance the youth scheme and gave it the measure of credibility it needed to counter the ever-increasing competition from the youth set-ups of other clubs.

Hixon spent even longer with Southampton than he had with Burnley – 20 years – before being attracted to the challenge of working with a North-east club, Sunderland, for the first time. Sunderland, too, benefited from his abilities through the signing of Michael Bridges, a 19-year-old centre-forward who was rated one of the most exciting young players in the Premiership last season.

Spotted by Hixon while playing for his school team in Whitley Bay, Bridges has even invited speculation concerning his chances of one day lining up alongside Alan Shearer in the England team. Hixon, who has been brought into Bridges' inner circle of friends and family in much the same way that he was by Shearer, is clearly intent on doing all he can to help the player realise that ambition.

Because of his friendship with Hixon, the same could be said about Shearer. Upon Bridges' Premiership début at Tottenham (ironically his favourite team before his entry into professional football), he received a congratulatory card from the England icon, and it is not unusual for Shearer to make himself available to Bridges when Hixon feels the teenager could do with playing or training advice and encouragement.

Like Shearer, Michael Bridges also fell through the Newcastle net. He had been at their centre of excellence for a while but had been hampered by injury, and as he had not clearly defined himself as a particularly exciting prospect, he was allowed to drift away. It was not until he was in his first year as a school sixth-former, at the age of 16, that he attracted Hixon's attention. 'People said to me: "Sixteen? Where has he been?" The obvious inference was that he couldn't be that good if it had taken him so long to get noticed,' says Hixon. 'This is one of the problems with the centre of excellence concept of catching them as young as nine or ten. The clubs focus so much attention on that, that they sometimes lose sight of the lads at the other end of the schoolboy age scale who might just have been late developers. Also, most of the important schoolboy matches are at Under-15 and Under-16 level, and once a player gets beyond that, the number of opportunities for him to catch the eye decrease considerably. I've picked up quite a few good Under-17 and Under-18 players as a result of this.'

Alan Shearer, though, was spotted by Hixon a month or two before his 14th birthday. So why was it that, while the scouts of other clubs couldn't make up their minds in their assessment of him as a potential top professional footballer, Hixon immediately took a chance. What did he see in Shearer that others overlooked or dismissed?

Hixon himself makes it sound elementary. 'There are certain imponderables when you're looking at a young player – his physical development, for example – but they were all quite minimal with him as far as I was concerned. The most important things for me were that he had a good football brain, and that he had all three of what I called the essential fundamentals – attitude, application and character. He was a winner.

'I can't honestly say that I visualised his being as successful as he has been. I was interviewed on the radio when he signed for Newcastle and the fellow asked me: "Could you visualise Shearer being a megastar when you recommended him to Southampton?" I said: "Look, Mystic Meg couldn't have seen it. If I had powers like that, I wouldn't be sitting in front of this microphone, I would be in a villa somewhere in the Caribbean." I don't think you can say to any kid: "You are definitely going to make it." There are so many things that can cause them to fall by the wayside or fail to progress in the way you feel they should have done. All I say to them is: "If you fail because of lack of enthusiasm or effort, things that you can control, you will deserve what you get."'

Hixon never had any doubts about Shearer on that score. 'He will always make the most of what he's got,' he says. 'He was playing for the Newcastle Boys Under-13 team at Benfield Park when I first saw him, and I was attracted to him straightaway. I thought he was quite well put together, without being what you would call a big fellow, and I suppose the things that struck me about him were that he was such a positive, aggressive runner, and had so much bottle. That's one of the things you look for the most in a front player – bottle. Scoring goals is not just a matter of intuition or perceptiveness; it's going into the box knowing that you're probably going to get kicked. You've got to be prepared to go in where it hurts, and Alan stood out like a beacon in that respect. He just came across as a lad with remarkable strength of character – and in my experience, if you have that, you're two-thirds of the way there.

'Anyway, I'm watching him in this match at Benfield Park, and after about half an hour, I thought: "Right, where's his father? I'm going to have an exploratory chat." Someone pointed out his father to me, and I went across, introduced myself and said: "I'm interested in your boy." When he heard I was scouting for Southampton, I am sure he must have thought: "God, is Alan

going to be a Channel swimmer or something?" But once I had
outlined all the reasons why the lad should be interested in coming
to Southampton, to both parents, I remember his dad just saying:
"Well, talk to Alan. He's the fellow."

'That in itself told me a lot about Alan and about the way he'd
been brought up. There are not many lads of his age with his sense
of independence. He was not precocious – he was just an ordinary
lad – but he had the ability to think and act for himself and, within
the normal parental constraints, his family were prepared to give
him the freedom to do it. I know that his dad discussed it with him.
But, for as long as I have known him, Alan has always been a good
listener who is able to absorb and weigh up different arguments,
and then be his own man.'

Having pinpointed Shearer as a youngster with more going for
him than a number of more obviously talented players, Hixon
arranged for him to take part in a Southampton trial at the
Gateshead Stadium under the supervision of Southampton's youth
development officer then, Bob Higgins. He, too, liked what he saw
of Shearer, who was promptly signed by Southampton as an
associate schoolboy just after his 14th birthday, on 7 September
1984 – a move that effectively gave Southampton first option on
signing Shearer as a trainee professional on their YTS scheme
when he left school at 16.

During the period leading up to this, his most regular
companions on his school holiday trips to Southampton were
Barry Wilson, his Cramlington Juniors striking partner, and Neil
Maddison, a midfield player from Gateshead. Both were eventually
signed as YTS players on the same day as Shearer – 1 July 1986 –
and, like Shearer, both were taken on as full-time professionals. But
whereas Maddison is still with the club, Wilson was released and
drifted out of the game as a result of a back injury.

Maddison, who was spotted by Hixon's scouting sidekick and
cousin Jackie Robson, and who was put in the same digs as Shearer
when the pair were taken on as Southampton apprentices, is
sensitive about his links with Shearer. No doubt wary about being

seen to reflect in his old colleague's glory, he is one of the few men to have been closely associated with him as a schoolboy player who have fought shy of media requests for interviews on the subject. When I tried, the receptionist at Southampton's training ground said: 'It's a shame that so many people like you only want to talk to him because of Alan Shearer – he is a very good player, too, you know.'

But when it came to the decision on whether Southampton would engage them as YTS players, Maddison was kept on tenter-hooks for as long as Shearer was. Hixon feels this was a deliberate ploy on the part of Bob Higgins, explaining: 'He was a typical Cockney, very sharp, and he had this knack for stoking people up, you see.'

Higgins certainly succeeded with Shearer. Hixon recalls: 'We had it in our minds that, under the rules, Southampton would have to let Alan know whether they intended to offer him a YTS contract on 1 March [of 1986, his school-leaving year] but this did not happen. Southampton were not showing any signs of having made a decision about him. As it got towards Easter [when Southampton were due to have all their associate schoolboys and trialists down to make a final assessment of them], Alan started getting quite edgy about the situation.'

Higgins, who is no longer with Southampton – he left under a cloud of unproven allegations about his personal life – has been quoted as saying that, from what he saw of the schoolboy players recommended by Hixon, Maddison was the one who impressed him the most. 'Alan was not necessarily an outstanding prospect then. Obviously, he had something about him, but the one who really stood out was Neil Maddison.' He said that he felt Shearer 'had a little bit more to do' to convince the club that he was worth taking on as an apprentice, adding: 'In the meantime, Newcastle were offering him this, that and the other, and his dad, a Newcastle fan, wanted him to sign for them. I hadn't offered him anything. We offer nothing to schoolboys at this club apart from honesty, friendship and a good working relationship, which is what Alan wanted and what his parents eventually accepted. But credit to the lad, though he was aware that we were not 100 per cent sold on him, he wanted to stick at it and prove me wrong.'

That final look at Shearer, and the other young hopefuls, took place at a residential teacher-training centre in the Hampshire village of Gurney Dixon. Inevitably, Jack Hixon, who was also there, best remembers the trial match on 3 April when Shearer, epitomising his extraordinary relish for personal challenges, out-shone everybody by scoring five goals. As the fifth one went in, Shearer, high on the adrenalin of clearing what he perceived as being the last of the obstacles in his path to an apprenticeship at The Dell, looked across to Higgins and showed him the five fingers of his hand.

At this point, a member of the Southampton coaching staff, who had been watching the match alongside Hixon, said: 'We'll be taking Shearer.'

'Thought so,' Hixon replied dryly.

CHAPTER FOUR

Polishing a Diamond

When Alan Shearer and his fellow Geordie Neil Maddison were Southampton apprentices, they lodged in the home of a middle-aged woman by the name of Maureen Wareham. 'They were great to have around,' she has said, 'but they cost us a fortune. We were paid £37.50 a week for each of them, but Alan would eat £50 of food on his own.' Shearer's appetite also extended to where he visualised his football career might take him. 'He was always very confident,' Ms Wareham explained. 'He said he hoped he would be a millionaire by the time he was 25.'

It would have been easy to dismiss this as a typically unrealistic teenage fantasy, especially in the case of someone like Shearer who had provoked little more than lukewarm professional appraisal of his potential and who was with a club with a long history of finding it difficult to hold their own in the top flight.

Lawrie McMenemy, who became manager in December 1973, did manage to raise Southampton's profile for a few years, during a period which coincided with the start of Shearer's interest in the game. Renowned for revitalising ageing stars perceived as being past their best, McMenemy steered Southampton to a remarkable FA Cup triumph in 1976 (when, as a Second Division club, they beat Manchester United in the final) and the League Cup final in 1979. At the time Shearer became attached to them as an associate schoolboy in the summer of 1984, the Southampton team, which included Peter Shilton, Mick Mills, Mark Wright, David Armstrong, Frank Worthington and Steve Moran, were basking in the glory of having finished second in the Championship, the club's highest-ever position.

But the euphoria was gradually replaced by a more downbeat mood. Southampton's performances and results in Shearer's first season as an associate schoolboy were only marginally less encouraging than those the season before, taking them to a creditable fifth in the table. At the end of it, though, McMenemy dropped a bombshell by leaving to take on the challenge of awakening the so-called sleeping giant of Sunderland, much the bigger of the two clubs in history and support, and was replaced by Chris Nicholl. Things got even worse for Southampton. By the end of the following season – when Shearer was taken on to the club's YTS scheme – they had slumped to 14th; and in each of his next two seasons, despite the stimulation of reaching the League Cup semi-finals in 1987, Southampton could do no better than 12th.

But Maureen Wareham, and everyone else who rubbed shoulders with Alan Shearer in those days, did not find anything to laugh about in his view of what he was capable of achieving. He did not talk about his hopes of being a millionaire at 25 boastfully. It was said calmly, almost matter-of-factly – with the air of authority of a young man with an acute awareness of being in control of his own destiny. For Shearer, that destiny revolved around his knack of scoring goals, an aspect of his game which he knew he could sustain at any level. Certainly, having got his foot on the first rung of the professional football ladder, Shearer was the very last person to allow what got him there – his obsession with seeing the ball hit the back of the net – to desert him. Thus Shearer, as a member of Southampton's youth team in the Second Division of the South-east Counties League, just went from strength to strength.

He picked a good time to be a member of that side, in that McMenemy's initial determination and drive in improving Southampton's youth system had begun to reap its first dividends, and Shearer had the advantage of being part of a sizable crop of promising 'home-grown' players all being 'harvested' at more or less the same time. He was one of an unusually high number of eight members of the group who were eventually taken on by the club as full-time professionals.

In addition to Maddison and his former Cramlington Juniors colleague, Barry Wilson, the list also included Ray and Rod Wallace, the younger twin brothers of the then Southampton winger, Danny, plus Jeff Kenna, Francis Benali, Paul Masters and Jason Dodd.

Masters, a midfield ball-winner and a former England school-boy international, joined Shearer in the England Under-17 team; they both made their débuts against the Irish Republic in February 1988, when Shearer scored the second goal with a header from a corner in a 2–0 England win.

The rapport between the two young players also extended to their relationship off the field, especially when Masters brought romance into Shearer's life through introducing him to his girlfriend's sister – Lainya. They married in 1990 and not long afterwards Masters became Lainya's brother-in-law too.

Masters, who was to be forced out of full-time professional football because of a cruciate knee ligament injury, was not the only promising Saints player of that generation on the same wave-length as Shearer. The same was clearly also true of full-back Dodd, and the jet-propelled Wallace wingers; like Shearer, all three went on to play for the England Under-21 team.But undoubtedly the outstanding prospect of these schoolboy signings was the extrava-gantly gifted Channel Islander Matthew Le Tissier. Two years older than Shearer, he had been signed as an associate schoolboy in September 1984 and as an apprentice professional in July 1985, three months before his 17th birthday. To a great extent, Le Tissier was a beacon for the likes of Shearer, in much the same way that the equally talented Ryan Giggs was for his Manchester United youth colleagues like Gary and Phil Neville, Nicky Butt, David Beckham and Paul Scholes when the Welsh winger became the first of the group to establish himself as a first-team star at Old Trafford.

The shining light that Le Tissier represented certainly did not go unnoticed by Shearer. For example, Le Tissier was still a YTS player when he made his first-team début at 17 – as a substitute – against Norwich on 30 August 1986. He went on to make 24 First Division appearances that season (12 in the starting line-up) and became the youngest player ever to score a first-team hat-trick for them – at 18 years and five months – in the 4–0 win over Leicester City on 7 March 1987. Trust Shearer to break that record just over 12 months later when he, too, was brought into the first-team picture while still a YTS trainee; at the age of 17 years and four months, he marked his full début by scoring all the goals in a 3–0 win over Arsenal. Even Jimmy Greaves, who had made First Division history 30 years earlier by hitting a hat-trick against Portsmouth when he was two months short of his 18th birthday, was edged into second place in the record books by Alan Shearer.

In addition to Jack Hixon, the other figure Shearer had particular cause to thank for this was Dave Merrington, a fellow Geordie well known to the Southampton scout.

Hixon had played a part in Merrington's own career as a professional footballer – he recommended Merrington to Burnley, where this heftily built figure with a strong personality perfectly in keeping with his physique spent the first nine years of his career as a combative, uncompromising centre-half and became a born-again Christian. To Hixon, the fact that Merrington was Southampton's youth-team manager when he started recommending lads like Shearer to the club was a massive bonus for them. After all, Merrington, forced to retire as a player at 27 (when he was with Bristol City) because of an Achilles problem, had worked for three years as a probation officer, so he had a deeper insight into everyday life and the pitfalls for youngsters than most men in his position. On the development of young players, Merrington, who had also worked as Jimmy Adamson's managerial assistant at Sunderland and Leeds, spoke very much the same language as Hixon.

Referring to what he learned at Burnley, he recalls: 'It was an extremely stable club. All the people who ran it had strong marriages and strong principles and moral and ethical values. There was a family atmosphere and players couldn't help but be influenced by it.' You quickly appreciate why Merrington and Shearer were made for each other when the older man talks about the need for people like himself to work on a player's 'mental strength' and 'strength of character'. He says: 'I don't describe myself as a coach – I prefer to be called a development coach. Maybe I am a bit of an oddball in that respect but, to some extent, I feel that when you take a boy you also take on the role of his parents. Also, there is much more to being a professional footballer than just football ability. Some lads come from bad homes, some come from good homes, but the bottom line is that they all have to learn to cope with the pressures of the game, and the potential pitfalls. So for me, you don't just cater for the technical skills of players – you also cater for things such as their education and what I would call the "inner man". They all have to be fused together.

'This is what I tried to do at Southampton. In addition to their football coaching and training, I also addressed things like the players' education, their attitude to everyday life and even their social lives. I wanted to develop the whole person, you see. For example, one of the things we did was to take them into local schools, linking the visits to our community programmes, and I also took them to the St Dismas Society [a local establishment for people with problems such as homelessness and drug or alcohol abuse]. When they first arrived at The Dell, a lot of the youngsters probably did not know whether they were coming or going. There were lots of strands to our methods and by the time they had all been pulled together, we liked to think that we would have a group of footballers who were pretty solid and mature individuals. As I used to say to the parents: "After 12 months, you won't recognise your lad."'

Merrington was a hard taskmaster, and he could even be an abrasive one. As McMenemy has said, Merrington, despite his religious beliefs, had not totally lost the fiery streak that had characterised him as a player and 'could eff and blind with the best of them'. As far as Hixon's prodigies were concerned, though, the support Merrington received from the scout was tantamount to being shown a green light. Comparing it to teachers trying to impose discipline on their pupils without getting the right back-up from the parents, Merrington says: 'All the boys Jack had recommended to the club had remained very closely linked to him, and I was helped by the fact that he readily endorsed all the things I was preaching to them. If anyone complained to Jack about me being too tough, he'd say: "Well, hang in there – it's for your own good." There was one lad who said I'd told him off for starting to get sloppy. Jack's reaction was: "Well, if you are, Dave's bloody right."'

Shearer himself was not spared this side of Merrington. 'There were a couple of times that I had to give him a kick up the backside,' Merrington recalls. 'He was such a confident lad that, just on the odd occasion, you had to pull in the lead and remind him that he couldn't afford to become complacent.' But he has no hesitation in singling out Shearer as one of the easiest youngsters he has worked with.

'When I first came across Alan, he struck me as being a typical Geordie; he was quite a happy-go-lucky, boisterous lad. When we were away, and the lads had an evening out, he fooled around as much as anyone. But whatever freedom he was given he never abused it. Even at that age he was mature enough to know where to draw the line.'

This was one of the things that endeared Shearer to Jimmy Case, the former Liverpool and England midfielder who took on a new lease of life when he joined Southampton in 1985 at the age of 31, and was their captain when Shearer was progressing through the ranks. 'Ever since I have known him, Alan has never gone overboard,' says Case. 'For me, he always had a good head on his shoulders – he was an adult before his time, really. He wasn't a stupid player off the field. I mean, I was probably one of the stupid ones early on [at Liverpool], although not *that* stupid – you couldn't be with Tommy Smith looking at you, could you? But Alan was sensible. A nice, likeable lad, you know?'

He was also a lad who appreciated that, while he had quite a few things going for him, ability-wise, he was very much a rough diamond. As Merrington says: 'In some areas, we tried not so much to eradicate his weaknesses but to build on his strengths. A lot of coaches don't altogether agree with that, but this was very much the way I tackled things at Southampton. In Alan's case, he was much better on his right side than his left, and by being encouraged to fully exploit this, the fact that he wasn't as two-footed as you would have liked didn't really matter. The example I use to support this argument is that of Ferenc Puskas [the legendary Real Madrid and Hungary forward of the 1950s]. People said that he was "all left foot" and that his right was used for little more than standing on, but when you look at his record there's no way you can say that this was a drawback to him. It's the same with Shearer. When he gets that ball on his right foot, he is liable to score from anywhere. Le Tissier's the same, but he doesn't have Shearer's power. The ball leaves Shearer's right foot like a rocket.'

Jimmy Case says: 'The first description that came into my mind when I first saw him was: "Power player". I was not the type to head straight for the dressing-room after training; I liked to hang around and help Dennis Rofe [one of the Saints coaches] in giving people any extra work that they or the club felt was necessary, and Alan was one of the lads I came into contact with the most. Dennis and I would stand on either side of him and throw him balls to hit into the net with either foot. Right foot, left foot, right foot, left foot – it was non-stop stuff, and he would have been out there until he dropped if he'd been allowed to. You could see how much pleasure it gave him when the ball hit the back of the net.

'The one thing I remember about him then, apart from his shooting power, was that he liked to hit the ball as early as possible. He would just sort of clip it, before a defender could get himself properly set up to get in a tackle. You see that nowadays with the number of goals he scores with shots that go through defenders' legs. You couldn't say he was the most skilful striker, but there was something about him that you knew was bound to stand him in good stead. Of all the youngsters at the club, he was the top man as far as I was concerned. In fact, I used to say to him: "If ever I become a manager, I'm going to come and get you."'

Of course, power alone was never going to be enough to make Shearer a top-flight centre-forward, and if there was one aspect of his game that received the most attention in his training sessions, it was his ball control, especially in situations where he had to take the ball with his back to the opponents' goal and a defender breathing down his neck. 'He wasn't a bad target-man, in that he had the strength to screen the ball and hold people off,' Merrington says, 'but his first touch needed to be developed.'

Chris Nicholl, the former Luton, Aston Villa, Southampton and Northern Ireland centre-half, is rather more forthright on the subject. He once said that when Shearer first came to the club, he 'couldn't trap a bag of cement'. He seems to contradict that now when he adds that Shearer initially reminded him of Kenny Dalglish and Mark Hughes, but he explains: 'Like them, he had a big backside and big, powerful thighs. That's why I saw him as potentially a top-notch target-man. People will say that Alan has always been at his best when you are hitting balls in front of him, but you've got to create the right situations for that, and usually playing the ball to someone's feet is the less complicated and more effective option. The first priority of a target-man is to be able to "protect" the ball and the way Alan was built made him ideal for this.

'As a player myself, Dalglish was the centre-forward I found the most difficult to mark. It was the way he used his backside and hips to keep you away from the ball. In fact, not only did he make sure you couldn't get the ball, but often you couldn't see it either. You thought you could get a foot to the ball and then, *bang* – his hip and leg would come across and would be shoved into you. My thighs would be covered in bruises after matches against him. Physically, Shearer had the same things going for him, and we felt it was a great foundation for us to build on.

'This was where the real work came in. In training, we'd keep hitting the ball into him, and it would keep breaking away from him. We had him out for extra practice almost every day, and I lost count the number of hours I spent throwing balls at him from every angle. But he would never give up – he was so determined to learn his trade.'

Nicholl could hardly help but warm to someone like that as he himself had been very much in that category. Indeed, during the early part of his own playing career at Witton Albion and then Halifax, the uncompromising Nicholl – never noted as one of the game's more sophisticated centre-backs – had to struggle to broaden himself even more than Shearer did. Recalling his initial spell as an associate schoolboy and then apprentice at Burnley, Nicholl says: 'I basically failed to make it as a boy because of a growth defect. The physical development of a schoolboy can be very erratic. When I started training at Burnley as a centre-half, I was the biggest lad in the class, but then I stopped growing and, having become one of the smallest, was switched to outside left. I was able to get back into the centre-half position when I started growing again at 16 or 17, but it took some time for me to catch up on what I needed to acquire for that position.'

In that context, Shearer was fortunate. 'He has always had the same build,' Nicholl says, 'and he has always had tremendous body strength.' This, combined with his insatiable appetite for improvement and his positive attitude, brought Shearer a total of more than 75 goals in his two seasons as a Southampton youth-team player; and it caused Dave Merrington to become increasingly neurotic about the possibility of Southampton losing him. The club, he explains, were great believers in their youngsters having at least two years' experience as apprentices before becoming full-time professionals; and although some players could have been viewed as special cases meriting an earlier promotion, the club were sensitive about being seen to have favourites. 'There was never any chance of Southampton not signing Alan,' Merrington claims, 'but you couldn't help but worry about it sometimes.'

Merrington became particularly agitated during a top youth tournament in Germany which, thanks to Shearer, they won. 'The tournament was hosted by Bayer Leverkusen, who had won the competition in the two previous seasons. We actually knocked them out on this occasion, and later their youth-team manager, who had the finances to travel around Europe and take any young player he wanted, was raving to me about Shearer and Maddison. "What is the position with these players?" he asked me. When we got back, I learned that Newcastle were on the scent, too, so I went to Chris Nicholl and said: "You must sort these players out now. If you don't at least tell them they are going to be kept on, there is a strong possibility that you'll lose them."'

Nicholl did take the advice on board, although Merrington, referring to the fact that few boards of directors are closely in touch with what is going on at the grass-roots levels of their clubs, still argues: 'I don't think even Southampton fully appreciated Alan's value.'

By way of example, he recalls the day that Bobby Robson, then England's manager, visited The Dell for a club function. 'Robson was standing with the chairman [Guy Askham] and I said: "Bob, this fellow doesn't realise he's sitting on a goldmine, meaning youngsters like Shearer." The chairman gave the impression that he thought I was joking – he just started laughing – but I was serious. I was not privy to what went on at boardroom level – I was just the youth-team manager – but even when Alan was sold to Blackburn, I'm not sure that Southampton truly knew his worth, and how much further he was capable of progressing in the game. You know, I just cannot believe that Southampton sold him to Blackburn without insisting on a percentage of the transfer fee paid for him in any subsequent moves.'

At the time of Shearer's move to Newcastle, Askham revealed that Southampton had asked for a sell-on clause in their deal with Blackburn, but that the other club had refused. He added: 'You have to remember that the fee was the highest-ever in this country. No one could have seen how the market was going to take off in just four years. We did ask but Blackburn would not budge. Alan Shearer was under contract but we were not in a position to be able to keep him. He made it clear he wanted to go and this was the best deal on the table.'

Leaving aside the argument that Southampton should have dug their heels in, Merrington says: 'One of the things you had to understand about Alan was his ambition. When I work with young players, I tell them that I draw a line for them in terms of the standard I am looking for, and once they have reached it, it's up to them to go on and draw a higher one for themselves. Some set their sights higher than others. You take Matthew Le Tissier and Alan, for example. Mattie is much the more talented of the two but he's been happy to stay at Southampton and be a big fish in a small pond. There is little doubt that had he gone to a bigger club, on to a bigger stage with better players around him, he would have developed more. But his philosophy is totally different to that of Alan. It is not in his nature to push himself, whereas with Alan it is. He had his sights set exceptionally high from a very early age, and the clubs he has played for – Southampton and Blackburn and Newcastle – have been more or less stepping-stones. I remember speaking to him at Blackburn and saying: "What's your next move? You've got to be prepared for your next move." Now why would I say something like that to Alan? It's because I knew that's the way the guy is made.

'Having worked with him so closely, I knew there was no way that he was going to remain at Blackburn Rovers for the rest of his career. I also knew that he would just keep getting better and better. When people talk about the potential of young players, they talk about technical skill, they talk about this, they talk about that; but the elements that I talk about the most are mental maturity and mental toughness. You can be deficient in all sorts of areas, but if you've got that mental toughness – the ability to handle the dressing-room atmosphere before a match, the match itself, and things like that – it can do much to help you overcome your weaknesses. This was where Alan was remarkably strong.'

As you might expect of any natural goalscorer, there were times when Shearer fell into the trap of being too focused on scoring for his team's good. One such occasion was a 3–1 Southampton win over Wimbledon in a South-east Counties League cup-tie, the week after his scoring début for the England Under-17 team in February 1988. Despite the scoreline, Shearer's team-mates complained that he had been too self-indulgent. Merrington was happy to endorse their criticism in the local newspaper. 'Shearer is good at holding the ball up and laying it off for the midfield,' he said, 'but he didn't do that and the other players found it hard to play with him because they didn't know what he was going to do.'

But Shearer himself, far from taking umbrage over this, welcomed the comments. 'He thought deeply about the game and was willing to take on the responsibility of expressing his thoughts to the people around him,' says Dave Merrington. 'One of the things I used to do with the players was to organise sessions where I would set them specific problems – mainly football problems – and encourage them to come up with ideas on how to deal with them. I wanted to develop their ability to think for themselves on the field and not necessarily have to seek advice from the bench if things were not going to plan. Alan was excellent at this. When we came in at half-time or after a game, he would be the first to voice his opinion. You know, if someone had not been pulling his weight, or had not done what we had planned and worked on in training, he would often point it out before I did. Some coaches don't like that, but I thought it was brilliant. Players who aren't afraid to criticise each other create a dressing-room openness that can have a tremendous bonding effect. Right from the word go, this was one of Alan's fortes.

'When you start to see things like that in young players, you say to yourself: "Okay, is this boy ready for a step up into the reserves, or even the first team?" As far as the first team are concerned, you have to see a hell of a lot in his make-up to feel comfortable about his making that jump. Matthew Le Tissier had done it – he more or less went straight from the youth team into the first team – and I was convinced Alan had the mental strength to do it, too.'

Towards the end of the 1987–88 season, Shearer's second as an apprentice, Merrington felt that the time was ripe to bring this to Nicholl's attention.

The Saints, who had started the season with no wins from their opening eight First Division matches to drop into 18th position, recovered sufficiently to quickly settle in the middle of the table. With a team which included Tim Flowers in goal, Glenn Cockerill, Andy Townsend and the veteran Jimmy Case in midfield, with Northern Ireland centre-forward Colin Clarke and Danny Wallace up front, they were not in much danger of relegation; but nor did they ever look like setting the championship alight. Even in the cup competitions, Southampton were an easy team to forget about. In their first Littlewoods Cup-tie, they were beaten by Bournemouth on aggregate, and in the FA Cup, a third-round win over Luton was followed by a fourth-round defeat against Reading.

While Shearer was going strong in the youth team, Craig Maskell, another teenage striker who had been signed by the club upon leaving school, was causing a stir in the reserves. Merrington, though, had no compunction about stating publicly that he felt Shearer had stronger claims to a first-team place. 'They are different types of player,' he explained. 'Craig plays off somebody, whereas Alan is a definite target-man. He stays in the game and keeps your forward line ticking over. You can build off him. He is not one of those strikers who is flitting in and out of games.'

Merrington's view was slightly misleading in that Shearer has always been regarded as being more effective when he is facing the opponents' goal than when he has his back to it. Nonetheless, thanks to his determination to become the complete striker – and Southampton's willingness to push him hard towards this – he was able to show he was capable of more than just scoring goals.

Merrington still vividly remembers the initial conversation in which he recommended Shearer to manager Chris Nicholl. 'You hit spells with players when you just know they're on song. It's like being a racehorse trainer – your sixth sense tells you that the horse is just right for a certain race – and I was absolutely convinced that Shearer was ready for the first team. So I went to Chris and said:

"I've got a boy who I think can actually play for you now. You're struggling for goals and in my opinion he should be in the team." He said: "Who?" and I said: "Alan Shearer. His form is red-hot at the moment, and he's the type who can easily bypass the reserves and go straight in. He's got the temperament and personality to handle it." Managers can be very wary about taking a chance on inexperienced youngsters, and the reaction I got from Chris was a bit sceptical. He just said: "Oh, aye," and it was left at that. However, I'd planted the seed, and about six weeks later [when Southampton ran into injury problems], Chris said: "The lad Shearer, Dave – tell me about him again." I replied: "Play him. You should have done it six weeks ago – he was even hotter then – but you've got to play him." '

By that stage, Nicholl was under increasing pressure from the local press to do so. An article in the *Evening Echo* on 5 March 1988, accompanied by a photograph of Shearer with the two other Southampton youngsters who had made their débuts for the England Under-17 team against the Irish Republic the previous month (England's Paul Masters and the Republic's Jeff Kenna) stated: 'Tynesider Shearer is the talk of the town after blasting 44 goals for Saints juniors, his last two coming against Bournemouth last week to strengthen his side's grip on the top spot in Division Two of the South-east Counties League. Hopes that his brace of goals would land him a spot in the Saints squad for Tuesday's match against home-town Newcastle were extinguished by manager Chris Nicholl, who feels it is asking a lot of the big lad, pressing him into a side scrabbling for points. The manager said: "It's better for young players like Alan to come into a side who can help them, rather than the other way around." That is open to debate. Saints need someone who can score goals, and Shearer has proved he can do that. True, there is a big difference between the South-east Counties League and the First Division, but it didn't stop Matthew Le Tissier hitting the target when he leapfrogged from youth to first-team level last season.'

It was at the end of the month that the Shearer 'seed' Merrington had planted in Nicholl's mind truly began to flower. On 26 March, with Southampton having scored only five goals in eight matches (and won only one of those), Nicholl had him on the substitutes' bench at Chelsea – a 1–0 Southampton win through a goal by midfielder Graham Baker. Shearer did not play any part at all in their next match the following week, a 2–2 draw at home to Wimbledon – but two days later, on 4 April, he was again included as a substitute, at Oxford; and this time was brought into the first-team action for the first time as a 61st-minute replacement for the injured Danny Wallace.

With the score at 0–0, Shearer could easily have scored in his very first minute on the pitch. An excellent Cockerill pass put him in the situation in which he has always excelled – that of being able to get into the space behind a defender, and running towards goal with the ball at his feet. He did everything right in the build-up, ensuring that he had avoided being in an offside position when the ball was played to him, and then knocking it on with his head and taking it deep into the Oxford penalty area. As the Oxford keeper came off his line, however, Shearer hit the ball wide. The miss became even more agonising to the player at the final whistle, with Southampton getting no more than a goalless draw against a team who were hopelessly adrift at the bottom of the table and who had not won a match for four months.

'Maybe the chance came a bit too early,' Shearer mused afterwards. 'The ball wouldn't sit down either. But I'm not making excuses – it is very disappointing to miss a chance like that.'

Nicholl, though, took a rather different view of it, preferring to focus on the ability that had enabled Shearer to create the opportunity in the first place. So, with Wallace's place in the starting line-up against Arsenal five days later thrown into doubt by an ankle problem, Nicholl made up his mind that if he failed a late fitness test, his place would go to Shearer or Rod Wallace, another Southampton substitute in previous matches.

Shearer got the vote – and the outcome was nothing if not spectacular. Some Southampton fans might well have been alarmed at the prospect of young Alan Shearer taking over from Danny Wallace. After all, the latter, much the more experienced of the two, had scored the only goal when the two teams met at Highbury five months earlier (at a time when Arsenal were at the top of the First Division); and even without their international central-defenders, Tony Adams and David O'Leary, the Gunners' defence was the last back line you might have expected to give a 17-year-old YTS striker any grand visions about his future.

Hence the number of raised eyebrows among football professionals throughout Britain after Shearer scored a hat-trick in a 4–2 win – the first time all season that the Gunners had conceded so many goals and only the second time they had let in more than two. The excitement among the Southampton fans was summed up by the *Evening Echo*'s Bob Brunskell in his report of the match. Under the headline 'It's a Grand Day for Alan', he wrote: 'Saints début boy Alan Shearer was the toast of The Dell today, flattening high-riding Arsenal with a fairytale hat-trick. Shearer took only 49 minutes to complete his mouth-watering treble and it left Saints celebrating their first win of 1988 on a day when entertainment returned to The Dell in grand proportions.'

Southampton's team that day was: John Burridge; Gerry Forrest, Mark Blake, Kevin Bond, Derek Statham; Graham Baker, Jimmy Case, Glenn Cockerill, Andy Townsend; Colin Clarke, Alan Shearer. Arsenal's line-up was: John Lukic; Nigel Winterburn, Gus Caesar, Michael Thomas, Kenny Sansom; David Rocastle, Paul Davis, Steve Williams, Martin Hayes; Alan Smith, Perry Groves. It soon became obvious that it was Shearer who was going to be the one to push himself to the top of the bill. Here's how Brunskell, writing his report during the match, described those opening 49 minutes:

'Saints had to look sharp at the back as first Rocastle and then Groves made adventurous runs. On each case, the cover was good, and the attacks broke down. Shearer followed Arsenal's lead and ran at their defence before being unceremoniously bundled off the ball, with Saints failing to take advantage of the free-kick halfway inside the visitors' half. Statham neatly beat Rocastle before hitting a fine upfield pass and Baker chased in determined fashion, forcing Sansom to scramble the ball away for a corner.

'Arsenal brushed away the threat from the flag kick, but Saints surged forward again to take the lead through début boy Shearer in the fifth minute. A beautifully measured pass by Townsend released Baker down the left, and he sent over a peach of a cross for Shearer to score with a downward header from five yards.

'Case checked another thrust from Groves before Saints pushed forward again with Cockerill hitting a deep cross to Clarke at the far post. The centre-forward succeeded only in lifting the ball back across the goal to where Shearer, caught on the wrong foot, dropped a tame header into the hands of Lukic.

'Arsenal equalised with a bizarre own-goal from Bond in the 11th minute. The Saints skipper, under no apparent pressure, chipped the ball back, out of reach of despairing goalkeeper Burridge. It was a cruel, unnecessary setback for Saints after they had made such an encouraging start; and it lifted the confidence of the Gunners, who threatened again with Rocastle volleying wide. Arsenal were taking control, and Rocastle was particularly prominent down the right-hand side of their attack. He swept over a low cross which Groves laid off for Davis to shoot wide from 20 yards.

'Williams and Townsend were having a bristling confrontation in the middle of the park, and Williams was lectured after dropping his rival. Statham curled the resulting free-kick into the middle, where Shearer rose above Arsenal's defence only to send his header past Lukic's right-hand post. Shearer was working hard, covering a lot of ground, hustling the Arsenal defence and endearing himself to the home fans. Thomas was thankful to slip the ball back to Lukic after being put under severe pressure by the young striker. But Arsenal were soon driving forward again, Smith neatly presenting Groves with an opportunity to test Burridge with a low shot which the Saints keeper touched away at full stretch.

'Shearer's début slipped into the realms of fantasy as he struck in the 33rd minute to head Saints back into the lead. The youngster challenged for Cockerill's pass, won it and sent the ball wide to Clarke on the right; and when Clarke crossed back into the middle, Shearer stooped amongst a forest of legs to head home.

'Williams was having a stormy return to The Dell. The former Saints favourite locked horns with Case on the edge of the home penalty area and referee Burge had to pull the two of them apart before giving both a verbal warning. Cockerill blocked a shot from Williams before Saints increased their lead a minute from half-time. Townsend rolled a short corner to Baker, took a return pass and crossed low for Mark Blake to wrongfoot two Arsenal defenders before drilling a fierce shot between Lukic and his near post.

'Saints, with three goals in the bank, suddenly looked a rejuvenated side and Arsenal were given a torrid time in the early stages of the second half. A magnificent run by Statham was spoiled when Townsend strayed into an offside position, but Shearer was the central figure in more drama and excitement. He might have had a hat-trick when Clarke found him with a cross from the right, but the teenager's shot was blocked by Lukic. But after 49 minutes, Shearer was celebrating a fairytale hat-trick. Clarke was again the supplier. His first cross was blocked but the second found Shearer, who shot first time against the underside of the bar, and then moved like lightning to pick up the rebound and score his third goal. Arsenal, one-time leaders of the First Division, were in tatters.'

Shearer, who had run himself almost to a standstill, was substituted for Rod Wallace seven minutes from the end, with a resounding standing ovation from the crowd ringing in his ears.

Later, Arsenal's manager, George Graham, attributed the defeat to his team being preoccupied with their impending Littlewoods Cup final appearance against Luton on 24 April (which they were to lose). 'If they think they can go through the motions, they are in for a big surprise,' he said. 'I've tried to instil in my players that they are playing for their places. The hiding Southampton gave us highlighted what I have been trying to preach.'

Case feels there was a lot of truth in Graham's apparent excuse. 'I am sure some of Arsenal's back-line players, if not all, would have started the game thinking: "Oh, they've got a 17-year-old in their team – they must be struggling." Professional players do think like that. The next minute, *bump*, Alan has scored and they are up against it. He himself really had the bit between the teeth as I remember. He could have concentrated on playing a steady game, but he knew Arsenal were struggling and he went flat out for everything.'

Shearer, showing the level-headedness and modesty that were to become his trademarks, did not overstate his case either. 'For the first goal,' he explained, 'no one was marking me and I was left with a free header. For the second, Lukic should have come for the cross, but he didn't, so I had another free header. As for the third, I thought I'd lost the chance when the ball hit the bar, but the rebound broke just right for me.'

He was less humble in the company of his team-mates. Indeed, when he and the other Southampton players were getting changed in the dressing-room after the Arsenal match, he felt no sense of embarrassment during a conversation with one of the senior professionals in telling the older player that he felt he could have contributed more. Merrington recalls learning about this the following week from Chris Nicholl. 'We were having a chat about his performance and Chris says to me: "What do you think about his personality?" I said: "What do you mean?" and Chris replied: "Well, they [some of the players] said that Alan came into the dressing-room and had a pop at someone." But Chris stressed that Alan hadn't done it in a nasty way, and as I told him: "I think that's brilliant. That's the sort of approach to the game that I am trying to develop in our young players." Some are better players than others, but with that sort of attitude, I don't see how you can go wrong with them.'

Among Jack Hixon's memories of that Shearer hat-trick is that, at the time, his protégé was technically a free agent. Hixon suggests that, but for Shearer's strong ethical and moral values, he could easily have exploited the attention his feat created by moving to another club. Hixon explains: 'The rules state that a club has to let a YTS player know in writing whether they want to sign him as a full-time professional and what terms they are prepared to offer him at least two months before the expiry of his YTS contract. But Southampton didn't do that. They had not forgotten because I kept reminding them, but they just put it off. Of course, Alan was still a YTS player when he played against Arsenal, and it was not until the Tuesday after the match that they eventually signed him. I know it's a hypothetical point, but just think about it – Alan had the opportunity at that point to say goodbye, with Southampton not being able to get anything for him.'

Not that there were any flies on this young man. Even at that age, Shearer was nothing if not wise in the ways of the world, and aware of his value to Southampton. Indeed, Nicholl recalls that the delay in getting Shearer to sign on the dotted line was due partly to the player himself not agreeing to the offer initially put before him. It seems strange that a 17-year-old should display such self-confidence and assertiveness, but Nicholl says: 'I was not taken aback by it, because that's the way Alan was and, at any event, I could relate it to my own experience when I was in my early 20s and been signed by Luton from Halifax. I felt so strong and fit – I felt that nothing or nobody could hurt me, that I could do anything.'

As far as Shearer was concerned, that sense of security was boosted by the knowledge that Newcastle were bursting to sign him. Nicholl says: 'Alan was an honourable lad – we knew that. When you dealt with him face to face, you knew what you were dealing with – he was dead straight. So, if you made him an offer which he didn't agree with, he'd look you in the eye and just say: "No, that's not enough." He wasn't the type to play games.

'What would happen in his contract negotiations with me at Southampton would be that I would make him an offer, he would have a chat with his father about it, and then hand me a bit of paper outlining what they considered to be fair. That's what happened when he came to see me about his first contract. I think he felt a great affinity with us, having grown up with us, and that there were lots of advantages careerwise in staying with us. But at the same time, he knew his worth.

'We knew that Newcastle had offered him a £10,000 signing-on fee and, obviously, because that was his home-town club and he had all his family there, we felt we would be in danger of losing him if we didn't match that. Then it was a question of our reaching an agreement on the terms of his contract. He did not agree to our first offer – he insisted on going away to talk to his father about it – and it did take some time for the whole thing to be settled. But the whole affair was conducted in the proper manner on both sides.'

Ironically, no one could have been more proud of Shearer for getting what he felt he deserved than Dave Merrington. As he says: 'On the one hand, I was employed by Southampton and had an obligation to look after the club's interests; and on the other, I had an obligation to look after the interests of my youth-team players, too. I would say to them: "When and if you get to the stage of negotiating a professional contract with the manager, just make sure that you understand your value."'

Still, he does not feel badly about that advice in Shearer's case. 'He did not need me to tell him that – he had the bottle to demand what he deserved anyway.' The young footballer also had the bottle to stick it out at Southampton for two seasons, under difficult circumstances, in order to improve his football education.

CHAPTER FIVE

The Dell Hurdles

Statistics can tell all manner of different stories, but what are you supposed to make of the fact that, in First Division matches, Shearer's scoring record for Southampton was just 23 in 118 appearances?

Despite that remarkable full début against Arsenal towards the end of the 1987–88 season, he had to wait four seasons, until the 1991–92 campaign, to emerge as the club's leading scorer – and, even then, his total of 13 goals in 41 First Division matches was not a record that would have led anyone to anticipate the phenomenal scoring rate the player was to achieve with Blackburn.

Following the hat-trick against Arsenal, Shearer had brought his total of league appearances that season to five by playing in the last two matches, against Derby and West Ham, neither of which he was able to mark with another strike. He played in ten games in 1988–89 and 26 in 1989–90, and his scoring records for those campaigns were nought and three respectively. It was only in the 1990–91 season, when his number of appearances increased to 36, that he could truly be said to have established himself in the side; but it made little difference to his scoring record – he ended up with just four goals.

One obvious explanation for this is that, during a period in which he was still developing and striving to knock the rough edges off his game, he suffered by not being in a stronger side. Significantly, his Southampton record contrasted sharply with the ability he showed at international level. By the time he left The Dell, in the summer of 1992, he had scored ten goals in 11 England Under-21 matches and two in three matches for the senior England side. Jimmy Case, then Southampton's captain, recalls: 'Chris Nicholl used to say to me: "We've got to finish in the top ten," and I'd say: "Well, you've got to keep the players you've got, and get in two or three more." I'd say that to him every year – "We need two more good players at least" – but he maintained that it would be difficult to get the board to agree to it.'

The other explanations for Shearer's slow progress were that Nicholl, his Southampton boss until the end of the 1990–91 season, continued to be wary about subjecting the young player to the mental and physical strain of first-team football at such an early age, and that on the occasions Nicholl did play him, the team framework – and the nature of Shearer's job within it – often tended to be geared more to the scoring potential of others.

Nicholl, whose list of centre-forward options the season after Shearer's début included Colin Clarke and the similarly experienced Paul Rideout (whom he brought back to England from Bari in July 1988) recalls: 'I was trying to do the job in a different way to Lawrie McMenemy. He had built a team with loads of experienced players who were approaching the end of their careers. When I took over I think there were five or six in the first-team squad who were well into their 30s. I am not knocking it because I played under him at The Dell and his policy worked. Lawrie had a talent for picking the right people and getting the most out of them and, at the time, he was spot on.

'But I think the problems of trying to pursue that policy indefinitely were shown by what happened to him at Sunderland where he was unable to halt his team's slide towards the Third Division and was sacked. I needed to do things differently, especially as the youth system Lawrie had initiated was starting to bring good youngsters through.

'However, there has to be a balance. If you're going to bring in kids, you have to have good, experienced pros around them. Also, there's a big difference between bringing a kid into a top-class team as opposed to a struggling side.

'The performances of youngsters do tend to fluctuate, and one of the things I learned from Ron Saunders when I was at Aston Villa is that if you are going to take them out of the front line for a while, it is much better to do it when they are on a high than when they are starting to struggle. Ron had a great knack with this – he believed that if you waited for a youngster to have a bad game before you left him out, the memory of it might be inhibiting to him when he came back into the side. This was the approach I followed with Alan.'

Under Nicholl, Southampton evolved into a 4-3-3 team, with the manager preferring to have at least two of the front positions filled by wingers. Initially, the players challenging for the wide spots were Danny and Rod Wallace and Le Tissier, and in a number of matches during the 1988–89 season all three were in the Saints starting line-up. At the beginning of February, Nicholl, conscious of the fact that his group of No. 9s – Clarke, Rideout and Shearer – were now in limbo, decided to loan Clarke to Bournemouth, so he could bring Shearer further up the pecking order. 'Having three centre-forwards and none of them in the team has set Shearer back a bit,' Nicholl commented. 'Hopefully, we can now bring him a bit nearer.'

The move, which was to prove the beginning of the end of Colin Clarke's Southampton career, produced immediate divi-dends for Shearer. Having previously been used in the first team on only two occasions for league matches, as a substitute against QPR on 3 September and Derby on 1 October, he found himself in the starting line-up for a run of nine matches. Then, with South-ampton uncomfortably close to the relegation zone, he was back on the outside looking in as the more experienced Rideout took over for the rest of the season.

In terms of the system Southampton were using and how this affected the centre-forward in their team, it is significant that even Rideout managed only six goals from his 24 appearances.

In a team with three men up front, a centre-forward inevitably has less room to manoeuvre across the width of the field than he does as one of a two-man strikeforce. This would have been a particular problem to Shearer, who was six years younger than Rideout and whose ability to wear opponents down physically has always been one of his major characteristics. Moreover, as the main job of the centre-forward in that Southampton team was to make himself available as a build-up focal point and to link the side's attacking play, the players flanking him – Rod Wallace on the right and Le Tissier on the left – tended to find themselves in the better scoring positions.

If it looked as if Shearer's style was being cramped, there was some justification for it. At that stage in his career, his finishing was not as clinical as that of his front-line partners. In addition, neither Wallace nor Le Tissier was as reliant on getting the right service as Shearer was; they were more liable to create goals out of 'nothing'.

Wallace, noted for his explosive pace, and Le Tissier, one of the most talented ball-players of his generation, were the leading Southampton scorers that season, and also in the 1989–90 and 1990–91 campaigns.

Nicholl felt that the three youngsters provided a perfect blend, a view endorsed by the England manager at the time, Graham Taylor, when he was questioned about the trio's international potential. 'All three are good players in their own right,' he said, 'but I just wish I could have them all rolled into one. Rod's game is based on pace, but he scores enough goals to be considered a striker rather than a winger. He has a lot of ability as well as speed. Alan Shearer is a good strong player who impresses me every time I see him. His skill might not be as great as that of the other two, but he deserves to do well because of his energy and commitment. And Matthew Le Tissier is technically more gifted than the other two, but he is dreadfully inconsistent. It will be interesting to see which of them goes furthest in his career.' If he had been a betting man, Taylor, a manager who put a greater onus than most on energy and commitment, would surely have put his money on Shearer.

A workhorse he might have been, but Jason Dodd, who joined Southampton as a full-back from Bath City in March 1989, and who went on to play with Shearer in the England Under-21 team, says: 'There is more to scoring goals than making a good final pass or applying the finishing touch. You also need people to make the right runs off the ball and unsettle defences, and this is where Alan was so highly valued in that team.

'I valued him as much as anybody. We were quite similar in some ways, in that we both knew our strong points and our weak points, and did not try to make out we were anything that we weren't. It was great for me to have someone like him at centre-forward because I knew that if I was in trouble at the back, I could just bang the ball forward and he would give 100 per cent in trying to make something of it. It didn't need to be a good ball to him – you could bet that he would turn it into a half-decent one, if only by putting opponents under enough pressure to force them to concede a throw-in or a corner. Sometimes, you would be wary of giving him the ball in a difficult position, and he would actually have a go at you. He'd say: "Look, you just put it in there – if I mess it up, it's my fault." He would work his socks off for the lads, even if he was having a nightmare game. So, although he wasn't recognised as the top dog in terms of scoring – Mattie and Rod were – he had every bit as much respect as they did from the rest of the lads.'

Nicholl suggests that Shearer, Wallace and Le Tissier, in addition to the camaraderie they had established through having come through the ranks at The Dell together, were helped by the 'education' they received from Jimmy Case. The veteran mid-fielder and team captain was certainly a help to them on the field, encouraging and cajoling them and using the simple, accurate passing skills ingrained in him at Liverpool to repeatedly bring them into the play. 'Guiding them through the bushes' is the way Case puts it. But, referring to the passing options that Shearer, Le Tissier and Wallace provided, Case insists that it was a two-way process; that the skills and youthful enthusiasm of the trio were instrumental in giving him a new lease of life.

Case, who spent six marvellous seasons at The Dell from the age of 31, was particularly enamoured with Shearer, which was some compliment to the youngster in view of Case's experience of having spent so much of his long and distinguished Liverpool career operating behind the great Kenny Dalglish. Case says that he was 'spoilt' by Dalglish. 'I could show you videos of goals where Kenny is coming inside from the right-hand side of the box, and just curls the ball into the top corner with his left foot. Alan wasn't able to get goals like that. Don't get me wrong – he's not far away from Kenny in some ways, but for any midfield player, having Kenny in front of him was the ultimate. Whenever he got the ball, he seemed to know where everybody was, as if he had a bird's eye view of the whole pitch. The number of times I would go on a forward run, after giving him the ball, and get it back from him in a position in which I did not think he had seen me . . . So, apart from his technical ability, his all-round vision was better than Alan's as well. But Alan, with his strength and directness, was good for me in other ways.

'One of the things that struck me about him in those days was his discipline. He was what you would call a very straightforward type of centre-forward, so that in itself made him an easy person to play with because you could read him.

'There would be a number of matches when he would repeatedly get into scoring positions but keep missing the target, yet this never seemed to affect him. Throughout those periods, he would never panic and try to make changes to his game in the sense of doing things he was not capable of. He was a percentage player – he knew he wasn't a Kenny Dalglish on the ball; even at that age, he appreciated that he had a particular style that worked for him, and that if he kept sticking to it, it would only be a matter of time before things clicked for him again.

'At that stage in my career, the last thing I wanted was to have nothing "on" when I got the ball, and have to hold the ball and fight people off before making a pass, because that's more tiring than anything. In a lot of ways, I got more help from Alan in that department than anyone. In fairness, Rod and Matthew gave me options, too, as did Danny Wallace when I played with him in the Southampton side. I have a lot of time for Danny – he was playing ever so well before his transfer [to Manchester United in 1989]. If he was standing on the halfway line, with someone close behind him, and I got the ball maybe ten or 15 yards deeper, the first thing I would do is look at his eyes. If they were screwed up, it meant that he did not think there was anything on for him, whereas when he opened them wide, he just went *whoosh* – all I had to do was play the ball in behind the defence and he was gone.

'Rod, being exceptionally quick, also gave me the option of playing the ball in behind defenders, whereas with Matthew, I'd curve the ball into his feet or his chest. But with Matthew – well, there were times when he could be quite lackadaisical and you felt you had to gee him up. I remember a practice match where I actually said to Chris Nicholl: "I'm going to bloody boot him." That's exactly what I did. I gave him a good whack from behind, just to liven him up and raise the tempo of the game. Sometimes, he needed that in competitive matches, too. When I used to give him the ball, and he laid the ball off in a situation in which I thought he could have tried to do more with it, I would make sure that he got it straight back. It must have looked quite strange because, even if I was half-turned towards the other flank when I got the ball back, I would check and deliver it to the other side again. The message I was trying to get across to Matthew was: "Look, you're a better player than me – you can do much more with the ball than I can." Occasionally, I would actually go over to him, dig him in the ribs and say: "What's happening? Are you going to beat him [the opposing full-back] or what?"

'Alan was different. He was fired up all the time, and we had a good understanding. It was very much: "You help me and I'll help you." Joe Jordan [Southampton's centre-forward when Case first started playing for the club] was the same. He was different to Alan, in that he liked to get the ball out wide and then head for the back post to get on the end of the cross, while Alan could make these surging forward runs to stretch a defence right out. But I thoroughly enjoyed playing with both because they were always moving for you – players like that are nice players to play with.

'If I got the ball and was under pressure, Alan would be the first to show for it either by coming short or making a run down the inside forward channel. The point is, he would invite me to play the pass which was easy for me; he wouldn't take up a position which would have needed a Pelé or a Diego Maradona to find him. He was extremely positive, too. Once you played the ball in front of him, you knew that even if it was a 50-50 ball for him, the first thing in his mind would be to end up with a shooting chance from it.

'As I said, he was very straightforward – there were no fancy bits to his game. I think back to Kevin Keegan – if I gave him the ball on one side of the pitch, Kevin was liable to take it over to the other side, beat one or two players, then come all the way back, beat another couple of players and give the ball to me again. In all the time I was at Southampton, Alan was the centre-forward who was probably the biggest help to me.'

During Shearer's initial struggle to establish himself as a regular first-team player at The Dell, he felt a particular affinity with Jason Dodd, who took over from him as the youngest member of the side when making his début early in the 1989–90 season. 'I think Alan was quite pleased when I came in because it meant all the stick he was taking from the senior pros – the likes of Jimmy Case, Russell Osman, Glenn Cockerill and Micky Adams – was switched to me,' Dodd says, laughing. 'There were two groups in the squad then, the senior players and youngsters like Alan and myself, and when we were in their company it was a question of just listening to them and not saying a dicky bird – because if you opened your mouth, they could easily slaughter you. The dressing-room humour in professional football can be quite cutting and I think Alan handled it better than I did. I'd come from nowhere – I'd been signed from Bath City whereas Alan had been with the club since leaving school and knew the lads. As in all clubs, the senior pros we had then would wind you up about anything – your hair, your clothes, your performance in training, anything. They'll say something to you that will make you think: "Oh, I'm in trouble here," and suddenly, when they see you looking all worried, they'll suddenly burst out laughing. Alan, though, was quite worldly at that age. Having already made his mark on the first team, he was more self-assured than I was – but he was that type of person anyway.'

Case nods in agreement, arguing that how young players 'handle themselves' off the field – and especially in the dressing-room – can be as important as how they do so on the field. He provides an intriguing insight into the culture differences throughout a club playing staff, and the ease with which Alan Shearer was able to bridge the various gaps and be welcomed into the fold of all factions. 'Even to be able to socialise with the senior professionals, the youngsters have to earn their wings. I think it was probably easier to do it at a small club like Southampton, where everyone is so closely integrated, than it might have been at Liverpool. Going back to the early part of my career at Anfield, it took a long time for me to be accepted in the first-team dressing-room – they wouldn't even allow you in there, they'd tell you to get out, all that sort of thing. Southampton had more of a family atmosphere.

'Alan was self-confident without being cocky or obnoxious. When he mixed with the senior professionals, he knew his place. What I mean by that is that he was respectful and didn't go overboard about himself. When you're trying to establish yourself in a team, and you're giving everyone the impression that you think you've already made it, it can easily have the effect of causing other players to shun you, even during a match. That might seem a bit strong but it does happen.

'At Liverpool we used to say that until you could buy a round, until you had the confidence to mingle with the senior professionals at the bar and stand your round instead of just wondering whether you should do it and allowing someone else to jump in, you couldn't be in the team. The point was that if you weren't comfortable in the company of the established first-team players off the field, how could you expect to be so on it? If you're shy, or in awe of what's around you, then it's bound to have an adverse effect on your performance.

'You definitely couldn't say that about Alan. Even at 17 or 18, he had a sort of presence; right from when I first got to know him, he struck me as being a lad with an old head on his shoulders who knew how to conduct himself. He got his first-team wings very quickly.'

As for team-mates around the same age as himself, Dodd, his room-mate on Southampton and England Under-21 trips, says: 'When we were away in hotels together, we'd do things like watch *Question of Sport* on TV and have a competition on who could get the most correct answers. There was no money involved – the loser just had to make the tea. You tend to have a lot of time to kill on away trips and, with Alan, whatever we did had to have a competitive element to it. As far as TV was concerned, we would even fight over the remote control and what we were going to watch; all silly things, really. But yeah, we had some good times – he was very good company.'

Shearer's level-headedness and sense of responsibility did not mean that he was averse to the occasional high-spirited jape. Dodd recalls an incident when he and Shearer were 'messing about' in the hotel lobby before an evening match against Sheffield Wednesday. 'We were having some soft drinks and I poured the little bit left in my glass over him. He went to pour his little bit over me – and as I put my hand up, the glass sliced my thumb. There was blood everywhere, and I think Alan was crapping himself for a while because he must have thought he had taken the thumb off. Anyway, he went and got the physio and it was decided that instead of going to the hospital to get it stitched – which would have meant me missing the game – he would do it in his room. He put five stitches in the thumb and, obviously, I had to play in the evening with it all bandaged up. I had a nightmare, especially with my throw-ins, but it was quite funny. Alan loved it, didn't he? "Get those throw-ins sorted out," he told me.'

This side of Shearer also allowed him to relate well to the streetwise Neil Ruddock, who had arrived at The Dell at the age of 20 following spells at Millwall and Tottenham. Born and raised in South London, the centre-half was the life and soul of every Shearer party. For example, one highlight for the guests at the christening party for one of Shearer's daughters, was seeing Ruddock embellishing his basic duties as the barman with a glass and bottle juggling act.

Shearer's friendship with Ruddock, though, stemmed mainly from their recognition that they shared the same drive and determination to succeed, the same willingness to go through the pain barrier. Indeed, the other players referred to the pair as the 'Bruise Brothers'.

In Shearer's case, the hard knocks – outside those dished out to him by opposing defenders – were few and far between. While his progress at Southampton was slow rather than spectacular, this was never likely to be a problem for someone with his doggedness. In fact, bearing in mind his awareness of his faults and weaknesses, and the need to be as thorough as possible in establishing the right foundation to his career, his slow development pattern was one he welcomed.

Nicholl's determination not to put too much pressure on Shearer meant that for the start of the 1988–89 season, the young striker had to be content with being selected only for Southampton's second and fifth matches, as a substitute against QPR and Liverpool. But he did get a run in the starting line-up from February, playing in eight successive matches in place of Le Tissier or Rideout, and he said: 'Everything seems to be improving, even my left foot, which I could hardly kick with when I first came here. My heading, control and work-rate are all coming on so I am quite pleased with my progress. But, having got a chance in the first team, I hope I can stay there. There are quite a few strikers at the club now challenging for first-team places, which certainly keeps everyone on their toes. I've just got to keep playing the way I know I can and be patient. Time is on my side.'

For this reason, Shearer would have been the last person to quibble with Nicholl's decision not to stretch his first-team run further, because he did not find the net in any of those matches, and Southampton, with only one victory from them, were just one place above the relegation zone. From that point, with Le Tissier and Rideout back in the first-team fold, the Saints won three and drew three of their last seven games to finish 13th. As for Shearer, the season ended on the low note of a cartilage operation at the end of April. But this was merely the prelude to better things.

Perhaps the big turning point for him came early in October of the following season, when he played in the Littlewoods Cup second-round second-leg tie against York City at The Dell. He had figured in their three previous First Division matches, as a substitute in the 1–1 draw against Crystal Palace, and then in a 1–0 win over Derby and a 2–2 draw against Wimbledon. But what made the York tie so significant was that he scored both goals in the 2–0 win that gave the Saints their 3–0 aggregate victory – his first goals at senior level since his hat-trick against Arsenal 18 months previously.

Ironically, it was a match that Shearer might well have missed. He had been troubled by an ankle injury, sustained in the first leg against York and, following the Wimbledon match, Nicholl told him that he intended to leave him out of the side for the return tie to give him longer to recover. 'I was quite prepared for him not to play,' Nicholl said. 'I told him he had done brilliantly to keep going, but that he should give it a rest. But when he reported for treatment on the Sunday [the day after the Wimbledon game], he said the ankle felt much better, and by nine o'clock on Monday he was banging on my door demanding to play. He would not give me the opportunity to leave him out, so for him to get two goals was a bit special. It just shows what guts and character the lad has.' It could have been underlined even more because towards the end,

Rod Wallace was in a good position to set up Shearer for a hat-trick but tried – unsuccessfully – a shot himself.

Not that Shearer was complaining. 'It would have been nice to get a hat-trick, but I am more than happy with two goals,' he said. 'Obviously it was on my mind that I had not scored for so long. It did not bother me too much because I knew that if I kept battling away, the goals would come. Even so, it was quite a relief when the first one went in.'

That goal burst was not quickly followed by an explosion, but the main thing for Shearer was that he could now see clear signs of all his hard work paying off. The following month with a further 18 months of his Southampton contract to run, he was given a new, improved agreement for the next three and a half years, to 1993. 'I am thrilled about it,' Shearer said. 'I had no hesitation signing it because I don't want to leave The Dell.'

His feelings on the subject would eventually change once he started to outgrow the club. But, at the time, there is little doubt that the enthusiasm he showed for Southampton was genuine, especially when he went on to become a more established fixture in the team, as part of an exciting attacking set-up in which he had Rideout as his striking partner through the middle and Wallace and Le Tissier flanking the pair. In a season in which Southampton finished seventh in the league, the latter two were again the top scorers (Le Tissier got 20 and Wallace, 18), with Rideout in third place on seven. Shearer, who made 19 full appearances and seven as substitute, got his three in the 4–1 win at QPR in October (immediately after the York tie), the 6–3 home win over Luton in November, and the 1–1 draw at Luton in February.

The 1990–91 season, though culminating in Southampton slumping to 14th place in the league and Nicholl losing his job, followed a more encouraging pattern for Shearer.

Le Tissier and Wallace were again at the top of the team's scoring chart, on 19 and 14 respectively, and Rideout was the next on the list with six. To those who judge strikers on nothing more than their goal-to-game ratio, Shearer's total of four goals, gained

in matches against Chelsea (2), Everton and Sunderland, was made
to look even more meagre by the fact that Rideout, prior to his
loan transfer to Swindon in March, made full appearances in 16 of
the Saints' First Division matches while Shearer did so in 34.

But anyone looking for more exciting signs from him as a scorer
could easily have found them in other competitions, and his
international matches.

As in the previous season, Shearer's striking potential was shown
in the League Cup. Southampton's first opponents in the
competition, then sponsored by Rumbelows, were Rochdale, and
for the first leg away, Nicholl selected Shearer in preference to
Rideout, telling him: 'Now go out and prove to me that I've made
the right choice.' Shearer's reaction to the challenge was typical; in
what ranked as one of the best individual performances of the
season in the competition, he scored two goals and made two
others to steer the Saints to a 5–0 win. As has so often been the case
during his career, his timing was impeccable; he was the player who
broke the deadlock just after half-time, and with Rochdale threatening to get back into the game, he made it 2–0 a quarter of an
hour from the end.

Afterwards, referring to his record compared with that of Le
Tissier and Wallace, the player said: 'It is a bit hard when they get
all the recognition and the goals, but it's up to me to keep up with
them. I have perhaps got to be a bit more selfish in front of goal.
That's not to say that if the ball is there to be passed or if one of the
others is in a better position I won't release it. Of course I will. But
likewise if I get a chance to shoot and I think it's on, I've got to take
it. At the end of the day, you don't get any recognition for working
hard. Goals are what count.'

And not just goals against the lesser teams like Rochdale. As if
to show that he could perform against teams at the top end of the
English game, Shearer produced similarly eye-catching performances against Manchester United in the fifth round. He got
Southampton's goal in the 1–1 draw at The Dell, and grabbed two
(one a penalty) in their 3–2 defeat in the replay at Old Trafford to

take his record to six in as many ties. Southampton reached the fifth round of the FA Cup, too, and Shearer's presence in their five ties brought two more goals from him.

But in terms of proving he could score goals consistently at a higher level – and, indeed, that he would play better in a stronger team – the most important thing that happened to Shearer that season was his inclusion in England's Under-21 side.

Wallace had already established himself in the side the previous year and, in becoming the next Saints players to get a call-up to the squad in 1990, Shearer and Jason Dodd might well have considered themselves fortunate that Lawrie McMenemy, Graham Taylor's assistant in the England set-up and the man who ran the Under-21 side, was still living in the Southampton area. McMenemy certainly did not need anyone to remind him about the qualities of Shearer, having been Southampton's manager when the striker signed for the club as a schoolboy. McMenemy would also have been aware of Shearer's scoring début for the England Under-17 team, and of his overall record for them of six goals in seven matches. But even McMenemy, who continued to be a frequent visitor to The Dell after his retirement as a club manager, must have been taken aback by Shearer's impact on his international squad.

In the seven months from November 1990 to June 1991, Shearer played in eight Under-21 games and scored 11 times. Those strikes included two goals on his début, against the Irish Republic, thus maintaining a record which had also seen him score in his first matches for Southampton's youth and reserve teams (and, of course, their first team); and seven in four matches in the Toulon International Tournament in France – two goals in the opening match against Senegal, followed by a hat-trick against Mexico, the only goal of the semi-final against Russia, and the final against France.

Shearer and Dodd first came into the squad in September, when they and Wallace were brought in for a match against Hungary at The Dell. Some cynics might well have interpreted this as a PR exercise to attract more people to the match but, as it turned out,

Shearer and Dodd did not get into the team, not even as substitutes. As far as Shearer was concerned, however, the impression he made on England's coaching staff in training made it clear that these steps could only be a matter of time for him.

Although McMenemy managed the Under-21 squad, he and Taylor initiated a system whereby different club professionals were appointed to help run it as 'guest' coaches. On this occasion, the man in charge – Oldham manager Joe Royle – was as impressed by Shearer in training as he was with any of the players who actually took part in the match. The day before the game, Royle staged a practice match between the 11 men selected to face Hungary and the rest of the squad, and because he was short of defenders, he used Shearer at the heart of the latter team's back four. Royle remembers it clearly to this day, recalling that Shearer won enough balls in the air and on the ground to suggest that he had been playing at the back all his life. Ironically, the opposing player for whom he created the most frustration was Wallace, especially when the little winger tried to bring colleagues into the attack from England's free-kicks and corners.

The following month Shearer made his first England Under-21 appearance, as a substitute in the last ten minutes of the 1–0 defeat by Poland at White Hart Lane, the first of England's qualifying matches for the European Championship. Then came his full début, on 13 November 1990 against the Irish Republic in Cork, that was to take him further out of those Le Tissier-Wallace shadows and truly start the process which would see him become the most talked-about young striker in Britain.

In a team which showed four changes from the Poland game, including the replacement of Wallace by Lee Sharpe, the youngster who made way for Shearer was Mark Robins, who was then with Manchester United and who had scored seven goals in six Under-21 matches. To say that Shearer more than made up for his absence would be an understatement. After 27 minutes, having had a header saved by the goalkeeper, Shearer pounced on the resulting corner to produce an overhead kick which was cleared off the line and then the decisive shot from the rebound that put England ahead. He scored again after 51 minutes with a brilliant solo effort, fastening on to an England clearance on the halfway and then carrying the ball forward to the edge of the Irish box before unleashing a shot into the top corner of the net. 'I gave it a bit of welly, and it was lovely to see it go in because it was one of the best goals I've ever scored,' he enthused. Only an awkward bounce stopped him getting another goal, after a Sharpe cross had eluded everyone in the box and dropped invitingly at his feet just six yards out. 'The ball bounced badly, hit my studs and went up onto the bar,' he explained. Still, in the aftermath of a show as impressive as that, only a perfectionist like Shearer would have felt it necessary to rationalise that rare moment of fallibility. It wasn't just his goals which made that match such compulsive viewing. Just to show that his determination to be more selfish had not caused him to lose his willingness to create chances for others his delightful chip over the Irish defence enabled his striking partner, Ian Olney, to make it 3–0 seven minutes from the end.

Not surprisingly, Shearer was now on an England Under-21 high. He did not score against Wales at Tranmere on 5 December – he was denied on three occasions by the Welsh keeper, Tony Roberts of QPR – yet he worked so tirelessly and caused the three-man Welsh defence so many problems that it suddenly seemed unthinkable that the team could do without him.

Again showing a refreshing capacity for putting himself under the microscope, Shearer was no less impressive later when discussing his learning process. In an interview in the local *Evening Echo*, he said: 'This is the longest spell I have had in the South-ampton side and I feel that has helped me more than anything. I am learning all the time, and the more games I play the more it helps me. I am learning when to make a run and when to stay put, when to turn defenders and when to hold them off. That kind of knowledge only comes with first-hand experience. I am not running around like a headless chicken as much now either. I was trying so hard to impress that I used to chase everything, which

Dreaming of the future

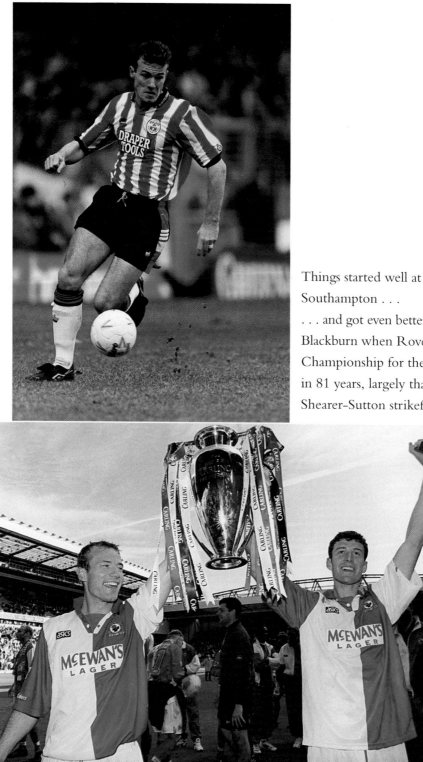

Things started well at
Southampton . . .

. . . and got even better at
Blackburn when Rovers won the
Championship for the first time
in 81 years, largely thanks to the
Shearer–Sutton strikeforce

Newcastle fans welcome the club's new signing

TOP: It takes three men to stop him: Italy's Cannavaro, Costacurta and Maldini do their best to foil Shearer

BOTTOM: Shearer surges forward past Georgia's Nemsadze and Shelia

TOP: Triumph for England in Euro 96 as their captain gets his second against the Dutch
BOTTOM: Shearer powers a header past the Polish keeper during England's World Cup qualifying match

Doing what he does best: with his head against Moldova (OPPOSITE PAGE) and with that deadly right foot against Sunderland

Acknowledging Wembley's adoration

meant I would tire towards the end of games. Now, if the ball is there to be won, I will chase it but, if not, I save my energy so I still have something to give in the last 20 minutes when many games are won and lost. I have grown a lot stronger physically as well as mentally. I feel a yard quicker and can hold off defenders. I feel a lot more confident now, and that has a lot to do with the manager keeping faith with me. We have had a few bad results, but he has kept me in the side, whereas last year I was in and out.'

There was further recognition of his progress in February when he was named the Barclay's Young Player of the Month by a voting panel chaired by Graham Taylor and including former England manager Ron Greenwood. Taylor said: 'I've named Alan on the basis that there has been a lot of talk about Matthew Le Tissier and Rod Wallace over the last two years. In the early days, when he first got into the team, he had to live with comparisons with them, in addition to competing for his place with Paul Rideout, an expensive buy from Bari. Alan can now be compared favourably with those two. This season, he has been given his opportunity and he has been doing very well. But this award is not just for this month, but for the months before that. It's an object lesson that you do get the rewards if you persist.'

This was to be further emphasised in more ways than one. At the end of the month, Southampton, ever more conscious of the dangers of taking Shearer's commitment to them too much for granted, added a one-year extension to his contract to take him up to the end of the 1993–94 season. On 26 March he was the England Under-21 scourge of the Irish again, this time at Brentford where he scored one of the goals – a close-range header from Wallace's corner – in a 3–0 win.

In the European Championship qualifying competition, England, having recovered from their opening defeat against Poland by taking maximum points off the Irish Republic, needed to beat Turkey, the other team in their group, in Izmir on 31 April to have a reasonable chance of clinching a place in the finals. On this occasion, though, Shearer's ability to rise to the occasion was

only able to lift his team-mates to a certain extent. He gave
England the start they wanted by putting them ahead with a header
inside the opening 15 minutes and, midway through the first half,
he looked certain to make it 2–0 only for the keeper to bring him
down as he was dribbling around him and preparing to shoot into
an empty net. The resultant penalty, taken by Chelsea's David Lee,
was saved; the Turks, boosted by the let-off, went on to equalise
and then take a 2–1 lead; and England, thanks to a late goal from
their substitute Kevin Campbell of Arsenal, had to settle for a 2–2
draw from a match that they should have won.

But Shearer, voted Southampton's Player of the Year by readers
of the *Evening Echo* – he scooped 54 per cent of the votes, with
Ruddock the runner-up with 24.5 per cent – kept going upwards
and onwards. With him in the team for the Toulon International
Tournament so, too, did England's Under-21 squad. Inevitably, by
this time, Shearer was becoming a 'marked' man, and England's
first two matches of the competition, against Senegal and Mexico,
proved to be major tests of his ability to withstand intimidatory
tactics. Senegal, having taken an early lead through an own-goal by
Paul Warhurst, left no room for doubt about the player they considered most likely to inspire a successful England comeback; but
Shearer, for all the rough handling he experienced from the
Senegalese defence, struck twice to give England a 2–1 victory.

Not surprisingly, this prompted Ray Harford, the coach for the
tournament, who was manager of Wimbledon then, to let it be
known publicly that he had become the latest member of the
Shearer fan club. 'Alan took a lot of stick but he handled it
superbly,' Harford said. 'He has a lot of maturity about him for
someone of his age. He knows the game and what is required. He
is a very honest boy and he is a good player, too.'

Shearer and Co came under even more fire three days later,
when Mexico subjected them not just to X-certificate tackles, but
also punches, spitting and even biting. Four players were sent off –
Jason Dodd and three Mexicans – and Shearer himself was
substituted for his own safety. But not before he had laid the

foundations for a 6–0 England victory with a hat-trick comprising two penalties and a close-range tap-in. He carried an extra responsibility for the semi-final against the Soviet Union in being handed the England captaincy, and responded to it as positively as those who had worked with him throughout his career will have anticipated. With the score at 1–1, and neither side looking like breaking the deadlock, Shearer struck with a volley that went in off the bar.

It was the same story for the final against France on 3 June, with Shearer producing another explosive finish – in the last minute – to destroy the host nation 1–0. He also picked up the two personal trophies on offer as the top scorer and outstanding player of the tournament, and the public praise inevitably reached a higher level than ever when Harford described him as English football's equivalent of the great German striker Karl-Heinz Rummenigge. 'For a 20-year-old, he is just amazing,' Harford proclaimed. 'He is just like Rummenigge. He plays like him and even looks like him.'

None of this, of course, went unnoticed at the next level of the England set-up. But for the fact that the player had an important date elsewhere the following Saturday – his marriage to Lainya Arnold – he would almost certainly have been included in the senior squad's 1991 summer tour of Australia and New Zealand. Little wonder that Shearer, not normally the type to get overexcited, appeared to struggle to absorb all that had happened to him since the end of the domestic season. 'Life has really taken off for me . . . it's all happening so fast, I can hardly believe it.'

At that time, Southampton had yet to appoint a successor to Chris Nicholl. Ray Harford was a leading contender for the post, which was further good news for Shearer in that Harford clearly knew how to exploit the striker's qualities. To Harford, it was important for Shearer to be facing the opponents' goal when the ball was played to him and for his team-mates to appreciate that when he moved deep to receive a pass to his feet, it was often just to create the opportunity to spin off into the space behind his marker. Thus, part of England's training sessions during the Toulon tournament were devoted to team-mates giving him the service he needed to make those runs effective.

Harford, who was to have an even bigger influence on Shearer when they worked together at Blackburn, says: 'In one game, Carl Tiler [the England Under-21 and Nottingham Forest player] came out of defence with the ball, but did not get his head up enough to see what Alan was up to. Alan was coming off a defender with the aim of spinning around the back of him, but Tiler just knocked the ball into him and the defender nicked it. Though the next day was a day off, I couldn't wait to do something about it, so I got the two of them together and we came up with something that we called the "Charlie ball". Basically, what it meant was that if Carl was in possession and Alan came deep towards him without shouting anything, he would get the ball short, and if he was going to get in front of the defender, he would have to shout: "Charlie".

'Dave Sexton [the former Chelsea and Manchester United manager and England coach] used this device a number of years ago, but he called it the "Fiver ball" because if anyone scored from it he would give them a fiver. It's a good thing for him that he didn't work with Alan, because Alan has scored stacks and stacks of goals this way.'

Having established such a close rapport with Ray Harford, Shearer could well have had mixed feelings when he learned on his honeymoon in Jamaica that the Southampton job had gone to Ian Branfoot. He can't have had any quibbles about the choice when he worked with Branfoot the following season – which would be his last as a Southampton player. Despite his dour image, Branfoot's ideas on the game were not dissimilar to those of Harford, and they benefited Alan Shearer more than anybody.

CHAPTER SIX

England Breakthrough

To Southampton's fans, Ian Branfoot was probably the most unpopular manager in the club's history. They did not have much cause to oppose him initially, especially as he was seen as a protégé of Lawrie McMenemy. Like McMenemy, he was born and bred in Gateshead. He was a defender at Sheffield Wednesday and Doncaster when McMenemy was at those clubs as coach and manager respectively, and in the early part of McMenemy's career as Southampton manager, he brought Branfoot onto his coaching staff. Branfoot then branched out as a manager himself at nearby Reading, thanks to McMenemy recommending him to the club's board, and had a spell as assistant manager of Crystal Palace before returning to The Dell (again on McMenemy's recommendation), in June 1991.

By the time he left three seasons later, however, he had the look of a persecuted man. Today, his Southampton career is best remembered for the fact that the local fanzine once published a front-page message which gave the impression that they wished him dead.

Part of the reason for all this was that Southampton came even closer to relegation under Branfoot's management than they did under Chris Nicholl's command. They did reach the sixth round of the FA Cup in his first season, but this was offset by their finishing 16th in the league, and the next two seasons saw them ending up in 18th place. During this period, Branfoot's chances of gaining a measure of popularity among the fans (and better results) were hardly enhanced by the transfer of a number of the crowd's favourite players. His appointment coincided with the sale of Rod Wallace to Leeds, and others who left the club over his troubled three-year reign included Neil Ruddock and Alan Shearer, who departed for Tottenham and Blackburn respectively a month before the start of the manager's second season in charge.

Because not all the deals were conducted with Branfoot's blessing – he certainly did not want to lose Shearer – it could be argued that the stick he took from the public was unfair; that, because of Southampton's failure to keep players like Shearer, the manager was operating with one hand tied behind his back. Unfortunately for Branfoot, he was not helped by his dour, arrogant image. This is where he differed from McMenemy. He did not have McMenemy's outgoing personality and suffered in that context in comparison with Nicholl, too. This appeared to be reflected in Southampton's football, which lacked the individual sparkle and entertainment value that had characterised his predecessors' sides. Branfoot came across as a simple and straightforward 4–4–2 man – regimented and functional, even negative.

Yet, for all this, if there was one man at Southampton with reason to be thankful to him, it was Alan Shearer. Branfoot's system of play suited him perfectly, as did the fact that the manager, like Ray Harford in the England Under-21 set-up, was willing to build his team around the centre-forward. This meant Southampton placing a greater emphasis than ever on 'hitting' Shearer early and playing 'channel balls' – passes through the gaps between opposing back-four players – for him to chase.

As Jason Dodd recalls: 'Ian Branfoot got branded as a "long-ball" manager as a result of this. I thought it was unfair because there is a big difference between a long kick and a long pass and, in fairness, he never told us to boot it. All he preached was doing the right things in the right areas, and playing to people's strengths. One of Alan's strengths was latching on to the channel ball and, under Branfoot, we used to do a lot of work on this in training. It wasn't a question of just hitting the ball forward in behind the opposing defence; we were given specific areas to aim for. When you say: "We have to get the ball in the area between the touchline and the edge of the 18-yard box," it sounds simple, doesn't it? But there's an art to it. If you play it too far to one side, the ball is liable to go through to the goalkeeper, and if you play it too far to the other side, it's liable to run out of play. You also have to play the ball early enough to give the player for whom it is intended a reasonable chance of not being caught offside. It has to be delivered properly, and I thought we did it as well as anyone when Branfoot was manager. It definitely worked well for Alan.'

So much so that, according to Branfoot, the number of goals Shearer scored for Southampton in his last season at the club – 13 (including one penalty) in 41 league matches, five in eight Rumbelows Cup and FA Cup ties – bore no relation to the high number of chances he missed. 'He had numerous chances that season, lots and lots of chances that he failed to put away,' Branfoot says. 'I think that had he taken 60 per cent of them we would have finished in the top six in the league. I don't think any of us could work it out; the only thing I could put his misses down to was inexperience. The bottom line, though, was that at the end of the season, we all came away thinking: "Yeah, he's smashing – he works hard, he's got everything, can't go wrong."'

That had been very much the message for Shearer at the start of the season, when his success in the Under-21 tournament in France had intensified the call for Graham Taylor to elevate him to the England senior team as a partner for Gary Lineker. With England's sights set on winning the 1992 European Championship in Sweden, Shearer was by no means the only striker under Taylor's scrutiny – others being looked at included Crystal Palace's Ian Wright, Sheffield Wednesday's David Hirst and Sheffield United's Brian Deane, all of whom had already gained experience in the team by the start of the 1991–92 season. Shearer, however, was the one who seemed to have the most to offer. Indeed, with Lineker having decided to make this his last season as a Tottenham and

England player, in favour of joining the Japanese club Grampus Eight, Alan Shearer was being looked upon increasingly as his heir apparent.

His future at Southampton was more problematic. Throughout the season hardly a week seemed to go by without reports of offers for him from bigger clubs and speculation about when the club would be forced to let him go. On his 21st birthday in August, he had decided to make a further commitment to Southampton by signing yet another contract, this one to take him through to 1995. It soon became clear, however, that the sale of Shearer was the only way Southampton could generate enough money to build a better team, and that other clubs could pay the player much more than he could get at The Dell.

At that time, Shearer said: 'I have already seen enough of the new manager to appreciate that he can do well for me and the club. I really believe this club can go places.' Not long afterwards, with Southampton sliding to the bottom of the table and other clubs falling over themselves to get their hands on the Saints' most valuable asset, Shearer and Branfoot were starting to take a more pragmatic view of the situation. 'It has been good for me down here,' Shearer said. 'I've been allowed to develop and learn and I owe the club for a sound grounding in the game. But whether I see out my contract, I don't know. I'm not agitating and I'm happy here at the moment, but the manager has said I probably will not be here the full length of it. He says he will sell me when it is right for me and the club. That might be tomorrow, next week or next year.'

For his part, Branfoot was well aware that it was very much in his and the club's interests to delay the inevitable for as long as possible. 'Alan is nowhere near the finished product, but he is worth a lot more points a season to this club than someone who is brilliant for 20 minutes and then fades or hides,' said the manager. 'He is a grafter who is full of aggression and enthusiasm for his work. Not only this, he absorbs things very quickly. With some players, you might have to tell them something two or three times before it sticks, but with Alan you only have to tell him once and he does it. So if you think he's a good player now, just wait – he's going to be an awful lot better.'

The feelings were mutual. 'I do like the way we're playing and I like the new manager,' Shearer said in the early weeks of the season. 'He strikes me as being very similar to Dave Merrington. He is very hard, but honest and fair, and you can't grumble at that. The training is harder – there's a lot more running – but it's enjoyable.

'I know I will be more of a marked man this time round because I did well last season with Southampton and England and made a bit of a name for myself. Defenders are going to make it harder for me, so it will help having someone alongside me. It is not that I dislike being the target man, but another [central] striker does help take some of the pressure off. I've always said it suited me playing alongside a central striker and I like the style the new boss plays. It used to be a case of getting the ball out to Matt or Rod, but Paul Rideout and I will have a bigger role now.'

Shortly afterwards, Shearer, having scored three goals in the opening five matches with Rideout alongside him, found himself in a new partnership when Southampton bought Iain Dowie from West Ham for £500,000. The underrated Dowie, a Northern Ireland international, might not have had as much skill as Rideout (who was sold to Notts County for £250,000 a few weeks later). Nonetheless, with his strength and determination, and especially his power in the air, he had done an excellent job as a target man alongside Tony Cottee at West Ham, and his attributes stood Shearer and Southampton in good stead, too. Like Shearer, Dowie had what professionals call a good 'engine'; the amount of running he did made you feel tired just watching him. The other element which put the two front men on the same wavelength was that Dowie was also able to take some of the scoring responsibility off his colleague's shoulders. He scored nine First Division goals that season, all of them strikes that brought the Saints wins or draws.

Still, even Iain Dowie will have appreciated why it was the other half of this duo who figured more in the newspaper headlines.

With so much conjecture about Shearer being promoted to the England senior squad, it was no surprise that on the opening day of the league season, Graham Taylor was at the Southampton v Tottenham match. Considering Shearer's penchant in the past for coming up with the goods at the right time, nor was it surprising that the striker scored one of his team's goals in a 3–2 defeat with a spectacular shot after only two minutes. 'One of the best strikes of my career,' he enthused.

He had to wait another six months to get the chance to show that he could do this at senior international level but, until then, he continued to be unleashed on England's Under-21 rivals.

Shearer, whose August birthday meant that he was still eligible to play for the Under-21s for another season, was given his first opportunity to pick up from where he had left off in France in the summer on 10 September, against Germany at Scunthorpe. Wonder of wonders – though England won 2–1, Shearer, for once, did not score. What must have made it particularly frustrating for him is that in the second half he broke behind the German defence only to be brought down just outside the penalty area with only the goalkeeper to beat. Still, this was only a friendly, as was the only other England Under-21 non-scoring game for Shearer, against Wales the previous season; and his claim to be seen on a bigger stage was fast becoming nothing short of overwhelming.

In the weeks leading up to the Under-21 side's next match, their penultimate European Championship qualifying tie against Turkey at Reading on 15 October, Shearer brought his league goals total to five in 12 matches. But as only two of those games were won, and Southampton were already girding their loins for a tough battle to avoid slipping into the Second Division, it was clearly a help to him to have reassurances that his club situation would not count against him at international level. 'Lawrie McMenemy keeps ringing me up to tell me to keep plugging away and that things will happen for me,' the player revealed. 'He told me I am being watched, and to keep my head up.'

The message was received loud and clear. England beat Turkey

2–0, and although Poland's win over Eire earlier that day made it impossible for England to qualify for the finals, Shearer gave his international aspirations another boost by getting both the goals in the last 15 minutes. So his record now stood at 13 goals from ten full England Under-21 appearances, which made him the highest-ever England scorer at this level.

After completing his Under-21 commitments in the 2–1 away defeat by Poland on 12 November, when he was handed the honour of captaining the side, his next step along the international road should have been the England B international against Spain in Castellon on 18 December. He was selected for the squad, but had to pull out as a result of Southampton drawing 0–0 at Nottingham Forest in the fourth round of the Rumbelows Cup and thus requiring his services for the replay on 17 December. Shearer, typically, looked for the positive side of the disappointment. 'The thing now is to make it [his absence from the England squad] worth while by winning the replay. If we lose, I will have missed the B game for nothing.'

Southampton lost 1–0, and Shearer's sense of misfortune was then compounded by David Hirst, the centre-forward whose style of play bore the closest resemblance to his, being selected for the B match against Spain and proving one of England's best players in a 1–0 win. This was not the first time that Hirst had seemed to steal a march on Shearer. The previous summer, he had taken advantage of his rival's unavailability for England's summer tour of Australia and New Zealand by playing against both countries. The same could also be said of Brian Deane, who also gained his first England cap on that tour, as a substitute against New Zealand, and who came on as a substitute again – for Arsenal's Paul Merson – in the B clash with Spain.

Thus, when Shearer and Hirst were included in a 30-strong squad for the B match against France at QPR on 18 February, and the full international against the same country at Wembley the following night, it was widely assumed that Hirst would be the one to play in the latter match and that the best Shearer could hope for was a place on the bench. The other strikers in the squad were Lineker, Wright, Merson, Alan Smith, Nigel Clough and Matthew Le Tissier, who was looked upon by Taylor as more of a striker than a wide man or midfield player, and who, like Shearer, had yet to play for the senior international side. Lineker was the leading First Division goalscorer among the group with 18 goals in 27 matches, while Hirst was in second place on 13 and Shearer and Smith were sharing third place with ten.

So, in the guessing game over Taylor's starting line-up, the smart money was on a central striking partnership of Lineker and Hirst. But Taylor, mindful of the need to find a long-term replacement for Lineker, plumped for one of Hirst and Shearer. It was a bold decision by the manager; Lineker had been virtually an automatic choice and in England's previous match three months earlier, his late goal in Poland had given them the 1–1 draw they needed to clinch their place in the European Championship finals. 'I have explained the situation to Gary,' Taylor explained. 'He knows I am just being sensible by looking at possible replacements for him now.'

This in itself inevitably put Shearer under enormous pressure. To fill the shoes of a player of Lineker's stature was a tall order for anyone, particularly against a team who had not been beaten for three years – a run comprising 16 wins and three draws. Wembley had become almost a second home for Lineker, whereas the only previous occasion Shearer had been there was when he was a spectator at the Charity Shield match between Arsenal and Tottenham in August. 'I just went for the day out, and it was one of the worst games I have ever seen,' he recalled.

In the media build-up, the news leaked out that Shearer's parents would not be attending the match because Alan senior couldn't get the time off from his job, and much was also made of the player's record of having scored on his début for all his teams, a feat that stretched as far back as his earliest schooldays. 'It's an amazing run,' he acknowledged. 'I can't explain why it's worked out like that, but I just seem to keep scoring on débuts. It would be a dream come true to get a goal at Wembley, but I'm not under pressure from the manager to do that. He has just told me to enjoy it, and I will.'

That was to prove a classic case of understatement: England beat the French 2–0, and Shearer again rose to the big occasion – the big personal challenge – by scoring the first goal and playing a key part in the second. As with so many of his strikes, his goal just before half-time came at an opportune moment for England, who had struggled to establish any real rhythm or create problems for the French defence. One problem for England – and Shearer – was that the French dominated the midfield, where Nigel Clough was unable to use his passing skills as effectively as he did at club level. Another was that the list of out-of-touch England players on the night also included Hirst, whose inability to get into the game inevitably had an adverse effect on Shearer's attempts to do so. Shearer, though not exactly causing the French to break out in a cold sweat, did look the more impressive of the two; and those with first-hand experience of that dogged, single-minded side to his character will surely have confirmed that if anyone was going to break the deadlock, it was him.

His goal, from his one and only chance of the game, was the sort of clinical, opportunist strike that was looked upon as more of a Lineker trademark. Indeed, the goal – a result of Mark Wright getting his head to a Clough corner, and Shearer showing admirable sharpness in turning on the ball and getting in a low drive – was almost identical to the one Lineker had scored in Poland. For the second half, there was another England lift through Lineker being brought into the action, in place of Hirst . . . and 18 minutes from the end, the potential of Shearer and Lineker as an England pairing became plain for all to see as Shearer dissected the French defence with a superb cross on the run to Clough and, upon Clough's shot from it being parried by the keeper, Lineker made it 2–0 from the rebound.

Having gained the edge over David Hirst in the young England striker pecking order, Shearer was confronted by another stiff challenge, this time from Paul Merson. While Shearer had to settle for a place in the B team for the match against Czechoslovakia on 24 March – a 1–0 win in which he was substituted by Hirst just after half-time and Alan Smith scored the decisive goal 15 minutes from the end – Merson made his first full senior international appearance in the A match between the two countries in Prague the following day. In addition to Taylor's belief that he needed to carry out as many experiments as possible before the European Championship finals, Shearer's apparent demotion was also rationalised on the grounds of the striker's importance to South-ampton for their Zenith Data Cup final against Nottingham Forest at Wembley the following Sunday. This, of course, represented Southampton's only chance of bringing a chink of sunlight into their troubled season, although as Merson scored the first goal in a 2–2 England draw, and Southampton were beaten 3–2, it could not have been viewed by Shearer as one of his best periods of the season.

As far as his England position was concerned, there was more uncertainty for him. He was back in the senior side, alongside Lineker, for the 2–2 draw against the CIS in Moscow on 29 April, but found it tough going and was substituted by Clough; and for the next match, the 1–0 win over Hungary in Budapest on 12 May, Lineker was paired with Merson – his tenth different partner in the space of two years. Taylor, aware that many might have interpreted this as a snub for Shearer, made a point of stressing that he could not yet decide between him and Merson. 'They've always been close. It's not a question of me now putting Merson ahead of Shearer. When Alan made his début against France and scored, then quite rightly he got the plaudits for it. But people sometimes jump to conclusions, which is not always the right thing to do when you consider that Alan's achievement was followed by Merson also going out and scoring on his début. I don't think there has ever been a wide gap between the two in my mind. I see them both as internationals of the future.'

For both players, the future included appearances in the European Championship finals although, for Shearer, this was open to some doubt when England took on Brazil at Wembley on Saturday, 17 May. Taylor, though not obliged to name his 20-man squad to UEFA until 1 June, said he would announce it on 19 May 'to put everyone's minds at rest'; and he indicated that 16 of the places would go to the 11 players selected for the team against Brazil and the substitutes. Shearer was not in either category; there was only one orthodox striker in the starting line-up (Lineker) and the one on the bench was Merson. With England looking badly in need of a stronger physical presence up front in their 1–1 draw, however, Shearer's selection was assured.

The next hurdle for him was to get into the team itself, a challenge that seemed to become marginally easier for him when John Barnes, deployed as Lineker's central striking partner for England's last pre-European Championship clash – the 2–1 win in Finland on 3 June – was forced out of the squad with a torn Achilles tendon. Taylor, who had long felt that Barnes was more effective attacking from a central position than from his more familiar spot wide on the flank, resisted the temptation to bring another central striker into the party, replacing Barnes with QPR's wide midfielder Andy Sinton. So, apart from Gary Lineker, Shearer's list of rivals was reduced to two – Paul Merson and Alan Smith.

Unfortunately for Taylor, few believed that he used these resources as well as he should have done. He has never lived down the controversy he created in England's crucial third and last group match against Sweden, the host nation, when he pulled off Lineker after 64 minutes, with the score at 1–1. England, who had taken a third-minute lead through David Platt, needed a win to progress to the semi-finals and Taylor had caused a surprise even before the start by naming Lineker as his only conventional striker – a strategy that had been tried, and not worked, against Brazil. As England were clearly labouring to penetrate the Swedish defence, you would have thought that Lineker, who needed only one more goal to equal Bobby Charlton's England record of 49, and was the

England player whom opposing sides feared the most, would have been kept on, with Taylor bringing another striker into the picture to give him more support. Instead, the manager stuck stubbornly to his system, replacing Lineker with Alan Smith, in the belief that Smith's ability as a target man would at least help England establish a greater attacking momentum, and lead to more chances for the players around him. It wasn't until 11 minutes from the end that Taylor relented, pushing on Merson for Sinton. But it was too late; by that stage, the Swedes knew that England were there for the taking and, just three minutes later, Tomas Brolin scored the goal which sent the visitors home.

Taylor's decision concerning Lineker was not the only one which brought him criticism. Many felt that if any player could have made a difference to the England attack, it was not Smith or Merson but Alan Shearer, by far the youngest man in the squad yet arguably the one best equipped to undermine tightly knit, experienced defences. He did not take part in England's first match either, a 0–0 draw with Denmark in which Lineker and Merson operated up front together. The second match against France, in which he took over from Merson as Lineker's partner, produced the same goalless stalemate. But, quite apart from his diving header which curved agonisingly just wide, his overall performance did much to help give the England attack the sense of direction and purpose it had previously lacked.

That he did not get the chance to do so against Sweden was clearly as disappointing to him as it was to his admirers. After the France match, he was quoted as saying: 'Lineker and I didn't do badly, and we work well together. But I want to be the one to get the goals. People say to me that I am one for the 1994 World Cup; well, I want to make my mark here in 1992. We have not played the way we would have liked to. People have been packing their defence and midfield and it makes it hard to score. But I have always believed in myself, and I am confident about the task ahead. If we do score, I want to be the one to do it.' Still, at least he had the consolation of knowing that better things lay ahead.

For Graham Taylor, the European Championship was the start of a decline in fortunes which saw him ridiculed as a 'turnip' in the tabloids, England failing to qualify for the 1994 World Cup finals in the United States and his own return to club management. For Shearer, it was the launch-pad for another leap forward, the step onto a club stage on which he could blossom further. His Southampton colleagues jokingly referred to him as 'Foghorn', a reference to his deep, booming voice. Yet, when it came to attracting the attention of clubs willing to pay millions for him, Shearer did not have to say a word.

All he had to do was to keep playing. That season Southampton had 59 league and cup matches and Shearer played in all but one of them – the First Division clash at Everton in April, which he missed through suspension. He put more into his game than most, so it speaks volumes for his strength – both physical and mental – and enthusiasm that nobody can recall his ever looking jaded. As a result, any club interested in buying Shearer knew that, even if he did not score many goals for them, he could be relied upon to give them good value for money in other areas.

At the very start of the season, it was no secret that Southampton had put a valuation of at least £3 million on him, £100,000 above the British record transfer fee that Liverpool paid Derby for Welsh international striker Dean Saunders in July. If Southampton felt that this figure would cause clubs to think twice about trying to take him off their hands, and buy themselves more time to to create a set-up which would give them a better chance to keep Shearer, they were in for a surprise.

In September Chelsea offered £2 million plus two players for him. Crystal Palace, having sold Ian Wright to Arsenal for £2 million, were also among the first to get off the mark in the bidding. Before long, the trickle of enquiries and offers became a flood, with Blackburn, Everton, Liverpool, Tottenham, Manchester United, Leeds, Marseille, Newcastle, Sheffield Wednesday and Aston Villa all throwing their hats into the ring. The Southampton camp tried to ease the pressure by raising their price tag on Shearer;

reports hinted that they had started quoting a figure of £4 million for him, and at one point, sources close to The Dell suggested that the club's valuation even reached £5 million.

Not that this dampened the enthusiasm of his potential buyers. By the time Shearer had returned from France, Branfoot's telephone line was red-hot. 'I'm the most popular manager in English football,' he joked. 'Everyone is being really nice to me because they want to buy Alan Shearer. I love it. My phone hasn't stopped ringing, with managers wanting to talk to me, asking me how I am and trying to keep in with me. They're trying to get Alan on the cheap, or trying to offer me players they don't want plus cash. I think I'll hang on to Shearer just to keep everyone being friendly.'

For Southampton's sake, if only it had been as simple as that. Early in July, Branfoot admitted: 'Alan and I have had a chat, and if the time is right we have to sell him. He hasn't told me he wants to go, but he has not stressed that he wants to stay either. From our point of view, if we can make our team stronger by selling him and using the income to buy new players, then we will. The thing is, it has to be right for both of us, not just him. Whatever happens, we are in the driving seat. Everyone wants Shearer because he is the best around, but he is under contract to us for another three years.' Branfoot was aware, however, that it could be difficult for Southampton to hold him to the agreement. 'If it meant that I could make Alan happy to stay here by offering him a new contract, I would give him whatever we could afford. But how long would it keep him happy when he knows that he can double or quadruple whatever we can pay by going elsewhere? He's never going to be happy because he has been away with England for a month, and spoken to people like David Platt who are on £15,000 a week.'

The player himself had been quoted as saying that there was only a handful of English clubs he would want to join, and it was reasonable to assume that these were Manchester United, Liverpool, Blackburn and Newcastle – the clubs which could offer him the best balance in terms of his personal financial package and his chances of achieving honours.

Though it had been Shearer's boyhood ambition to play for Newcastle, and though his home-town club were managed by his old idol Kevin Keegan, the attraction of going back to his football roots was offset by the club not being in the newly formed Premier League. Initially, he would also have considered this a big minus point against Blackburn, who, according to Branfoot, were the only club to make a firm offer for Shearer during the 1991–92 season. Blackburn, of course, ended the campaign by clinching promotion and, with the lavish patronage of their benefactor Jack Walker, a manager of the stature of Kenny Dalglish and a coach as highly respected by Shearer as Ray Harford, the close season saw Rovers rise to the top of the pile of would-be Shearer purchasers.

Money was really no object to Blackburn then, so much so that even Manchester United and Liverpool were taken aback by what the newly promoted club were prepared to fork out in transfer fees and salaries.

This seemed surprising in the case of United, the English club who generated the biggest income. But having become a PLC, they applied a more hard-headed business approach to the game than other clubs and because of their sensitivity about their image in the City, were loath to do anything which might be construed as being financially imprudent. Even for Shearer, there was a limit to how far their manager, Alex Ferguson, could go, especially as the period of the transfer saga coincided with United having undertaken costly ground improvement work in preparation for the use of Old Trafford for Euro 96 matches, and the club were preparing to release their accounts for the previous financial year to their shareholders.

So, in his quest for the player, Ferguson was forced to curb his impulsive nature and play a more patient game. In contrast, Dalglish, in a much more simple and straightforward set-up than Ferguson, and with a man like Jack Walker happy to give him virtually whatever he deemed necessary to make Blackburn a power in the game again, could be as gung-ho in such matters as he wished.

Alhough Ferguson was reported to have been unwilling to pay more than £3.2 million for Shearer (Blackburn topped that by including the transfer of the £400,000-rated David Speedie as part of the deal), this was of less concern to him than the salary with which Blackburn tempted the player. Ferguson took the view that to match them in that department (Shearer was reportedly paid a signing-on fee of around £500,000 and given a four-year contract worth £2 million) would force his own club to raise their wage structure to an unacceptable level.

That Manchester United lost out in the race for Shearer was clearly difficult for Alex Ferguson to accept, especially as the club were widely acknowledged to be at the head of the queue for him throughout the season and that their need of a player of his calibre was emphasised by their finishing runners-up to Leeds United in the Championship.

It is believed that United made their first official move for Shearer immediately after the striker had led the Saints to victory over them in a fourth-round FA Cup replay at The Dell. It was a tremendous night for Shearer, who scored the goal that brought Southampton level at 2–2, and was again on the scoresheet as they clinched a 4–2 win on penalties. Later, the possibility of United signing Shearer was discussed by directors of the two clubs in the boardroom. United were told that Southampton would not even consider selling the player until the summer, but as England's most glamorous club they must have felt that this in itself would be a considerable advantage to them in any future battle for his signature.

The relationship between the two clubs – or at least between the two managers – took on a rather different complexion when United beat Southampton 1–0 at home in the league on 16 April. Southampton made it a tough, frustrating struggle for United, packing their defence and producing a surprisingly high level of commitment for a team who had just ensured their First Division survival. At the final whistle, when Branfoot approached Ferguson to shake his hand, a hyped-up Fergie told him: 'If you think you can shake hands with me after coming here and playing like that, you can ★★★★ off.'

Ferguson later apologised for his outburst but would be involved in another controversy – this time one in which Shearer was directly involved – over his reported comments about the striker's decision to join Blackburn in a United video in November 1995. 'I was disappointed in my conversations with him,' Ferguson was quoted as saying. 'He surprised me. It seemed that money was the most important thing to him. There wasn't anything I could do at that point, to be honest.' There was some confusion over this issue because Shearer has said: 'Ian Branfoot told me Southampton had come close to agreeing a fee [with United] and that it was then up to me to talk to Alex Ferguson. But I never actually got that far. I talked with Blackburn and that was it. It was pure instinct, a gut feeling. I had to move to Ewood.'

The idea that Shearer had put money before professional considerations was a common view at the time of his transfer. Mel Stein, then his agent, was quoted in the *Daily Star* as saying: 'Blackburn are in the Premiership, they have Kenny Dalglish as manager, they have Jack Walker as benefactor . . . and they have incredible development plans. I call that a big club.' In an article in the Southampton *Evening Echo*, the player himself said: 'People just think I have gone for the money, but if that was the case I would have gone abroad. I do not think the time was right for me or my wife Lainya to go abroad, especially with our first baby due in September. I am still only 21, so there is plenty of time for that in the future. I am ambitious, and that's why I went to Blackburn – because I think they are going places.'

For a few hours, it looked as if he might not be going to Rovers after all, as a result of David Speedie causing a hitch in the deal by not being able to reach agreement on his own terms. It is believed that Blackburn overcame that problem by giving him a 'signing-off' fee, and Shearer put pen to paper with the club on 25 July.

Alex Ferguson, who had made David Hirst his No. 2 target, did not get him either. The Sheffield Wednesday striker might well have found himself at Old Trafford the following season but for the fact that he missed two large chunks of it because of injury. United, having bought Eric Cantona from Leeds, went on to win the Championship for the first time in 26 years.

Southampton, too, started the season with a new look in attack, with Speedie joining forces again with his former Chelsea colleague Kerry Dixon. 'The money received from Shearer has enabled me to buy two proven experienced internationals who have played together and who can add much to the attacking prowess of the club,' Branfoot said at the time. But Dixon played in only nine league matches and scored no more than two goals, while Speedie, who made just two appearances more, did not get any. Le Tissier with 15 and Dowie with 11 did well enough, but once again Southampton were involved in a relegation struggle.

Today, Ian Branfoot, Director of Football at Fulham, admits that he would rather have sold Le Tissier than Shearer. Though Le Tissier's goals have done much to keep Southampton in the top flight for so long, the club's former manager argues that Shearer would have been the more effective of the two in his overall influence on the team.

Of course, Shearer, unlike Le Tissier, was never going to be content to spend the rest of his career at The Dell. 'Not many people have Shearer's drive and ambition,' Branfoot points out. Nonetheless, when looking at what has happened to Southampton since Shearer's departure, he says, 'A lot of people said at the time that it was a good deal for the club, and in a way it was. I think Kenny Dalglish got some stick for paying what he did for Alan, and as far as we were concerned the bonus was that Blackburn were willing to pay the whole £3 million or so straightaway – usually, it would have been 50 per cent down and the rest in instalments. I couldn't have done anything about it; I was told by the board to sell Alan, and they were the ones who did the deal. There was no question about it. I was told: "We're selling him," and that was it.

It made sense financially, but football-wise . . . well, how do you replace someone like Alan Shearer?

'It's not just his goals that make him such an influential player, it's also his approach to the game. You know, when I think of Shearer, the first thing I remember is a match where the opposition had the ball deep in their half, and Alan tried to stop them from getting it out of that area. He made a run from the middle to the flank to stop their right back going forward with the ball and then, when the right-back played it across to the left-back, Alan burst over to that side and was chasing him almost to the halfway line. When you put that together with his self-confidence and his scoring ability, it's impossible to exaggerate how much of a loss he was to Southampton.

'You have to be a manager to fully appreciate the feeling that goes through a dressing-room when someone like that is not there. In a strange sort of way, if I could have paid Alan four times more than the other players were getting – which I couldn't – I don't think they would have bothered too much. If anything, I think they would have been bothered more about Matthew Le Tissier getting four times more than them. You just cannot replace an Alan Shearer unless you are exceptionally lucky or have pots of money.'

Neither factor applied to Branfoot, who was sacked two seasons later. Losing Shearer in no way lessened his respect and admiration for the player. He was just grateful for the experience of having worked with him – a feeling shared by everyone who came into contact with Shearer at Southampton.

Indeed, when he left for Blackburn, his popularity in the city both as a person and as a footballer was encapsulated by an unusual – and moving – editorial in the *Evening Echo*. Under the headline 'All the best, Alan', it stated: 'All Saints fans will feel a great loss with the parting of striker Alan Shearer to Blackburn Rovers. Alan has grown up with the club and become an essential part of The Dell set-up. Now he has gone on to pastures new in the knowledge that he is the highest-paid player in the country. He has a massive weight on his shoulders, but he starts with his new club knowing that he has this city's best wishes going with him. Alan Shearer has always conducted himself well, and has shown a maturity beyond his years. The sports team at this newspaper and the supporters at The Dell have had a great relationship with him. We would like to thank him for all he has done for sport in this area and we are confident that he will go on to even greater things.'

CHAPTER SEVEN

Harford's Help

Ray Harford looks back on his five years at Blackburn – as assistant manager and then manager – as the most stimulating football 'adventure' of his life. One of the main reasons was that for most of this period, Harford again worked closely with Alan Shearer.

This is not to minimise the part that Jack Walker and Kenny Dalglish played in Harford achieving fulfilment. The excitement he experienced with Blackburn's stunning rise from the middle of the old First Division to the top of the Premiership certainly would not have been possible without Walker's patronage. The 68-year-old Walker, born and bred in Blackburn, and one of Britain's richest men, had long clung to the dream of Rovers becoming a force in football again. Having accumulated a personal fortune estimated at £500 million – thanks largely to the sale of the family steel business to British Steel for £330 million in 1989 – he backed his dream with hard cash. The £60 million he poured into the club, one half of which was spent on players' transfer fees and wages, and the remainder on rebuilding the stadium, set an agenda that no club in Britain could compete with. In being part of such a powerful and glamorous operation, Harford was also fortunate to rub shoulders with a manager of the stature of Kenny Dalglish, a man whose charisma prompted players to sign for him rather than for the club, a man of whom even the most accomplished players were in awe and a man who had an innate appreciation of what made great teams tick.

On the field, though, it was Shearer who made the big difference to Blackburn. Harford, an outstanding coach who worked with him and the rest of the players each day on the 'shop floor' of the training ground, found the job absorbing to say the least.

The relationship between the two men was particularly close. The pair had already established an effective rapport in the summer of 1991 when Harford, then Wimbledon's manager, was Shearer's England Under-21 team coach in France. For Harford it was 'love' at first sight mainly because of Shearer's level-headedness and commitment. Harford was bound to admire this side of the player as much as anyone because Shearer's working-class approach to the game had been a prominent feature in Harford himself during his own playing career as a middle-of-the-road centre-half with Charlton, Exeter, Lincoln, Mansfield, Port Vale and Colchester.

The work ethic – especially when applied to teams hiding individual flaws through perfecting their system or pattern of play – remained an integral part of his methods as a coach or manager at Colchester, Fulham, Luton and Wimbledon. His philosophy helped bring out the best in a number of players, notably at Fulham (where he was the first-team coach when they gained promotion from the Third Division in 1980) and Luton (where he was manager of their surprise 1988 League Cup-winning side).

In terms of working relationships, Shearer was the player with whom he felt most compatible. 'I fell in love with him, absolutely fell in love with him,' Harford recalls. So it was no surprise that he made Shearer captain of the England Under-21 team in France, and that upon joining forces with Dalglish at Blackburn four months later, he wasted no time in advising his partner to pull out all the stops to bring the player to Ewood Park, even though Shearer had confided to him in France that if he moved from Southampton it would have to be to a Premiership club. In view of the money available to Dalglish in the transfer market, which had immediately enabled him to twice break Blackburn's transfer fee record by signing centre-half Colin Hendry (Manchester City) for £700,000 and striker Mike Newell (Everton) for £1.1 million in

November, it was worth a try. In any event, once Blackburn clinched their place in the Premiership at the end of the season, thanks to a 1–0 win over Leicester in the play-off final at Wembley, Harford always felt that his rapport with Shearer, combined with Walker's financial backing and Dalglish's image, would win the day for them. 'I was always very confident he was going to come to us,' he recalls. 'I can't explain the reason; it was just a gut feeling.'

When it came to Shearer fulfilling his potential at Blackburn, the relationship between Harford and Dalglish was no less important than Harford's rapport with the player. Dalglish was nothing if not astute in luring Harford to Blackburn when he joined the club in October 1991; he did not have Harford's coaching ability – in the sense of being able to organise training sessions and pay the necessary attention to every technical detail in team practices – and needed someone who could complement his own skills. In the main, they gelled exceptionally well; in addition to their mutual respect, they liked each other as people. But, as might be expected of two men who came from different sides of the football tracks, Harford and Dalglish differed in their ideas on how the game should be played.

Dalglish's Liverpool had been a passing team, renowned for building attacks patiently from the back; Harford, on the other hand, leaned towards a more straightforward approach on the grounds that 'fans will only accept their team playing it around at the back if the side are winning'. His philosophy originated to some extent from a match between the Colchester team he coached and Graham Taylor's Watford some years earlier. 'We were trying to play possession football, but they got the ball, it went straight from one end of the field to the other and we were 1–0 down. Later, I said to Graham: "You know, we're finding it difficult to educate the crowd in our way of playing," and he said: "They are not coming to be educated – they are coming to be entertained." I never ever forgot that, because basically he was right. What he was saying was that you have to get the ball into the last third. The way you do it does not need to be pretty on the eye – what matters is that you are getting the ball into areas from which you can score.'

This was music to the ears of Alan Shearer who, in common with most goalscorers, thrived on 'early' balls, and not having to make too many fruitless runs to gain possession. Dalglish was enthusiastic.

To Dalglish, Harford's approach appeared to be too disciplined and regimented, and did not allow players enough scope to express their individuality; to Harford, Dalglish, being the football genius that he was, was inclined to lose sight of the fact that precious few players were capable of doing what he did and that his methods left too much to chance. The pair would often have long debates on the subject, with Dalglish using his old Liverpool team as an example of a group of players who had benefited from not being subjected to a lot of coaching, and Harford arguing that Dalglish, a man apart even at Anfield, was probably too blinkered on that side of the game to be fully tuned in to the work some players required.

Some of their discussions would have kept scholars of the game's finer technical points absorbed for hours. Their players, too, gained much from them. As Shearer's fellow striker, Mike Newell, says: 'You don't want your manager and coach agreeing on every subject, do you? Kenny and Ray never fell out over anything, and one of the great things about having them together was that you got the best of both worlds.

'Kenny just wanted to pick his team and let them get on with it. He would tell you little things, either in training or in a match, and if he could see things weren't going right for you he would tell you how he thought you might change it around. He focused on you as an individual, on your individual ability, whereas Ray dealt with the collective side of things more, the way we functioned as a team. Kenny knew his limitations – he knew he wasn't a coach – and that's where Ray came in.'

One example of the contrast between Harford and Dalglish concerned Harford's insistence that when the striker had his back to the opposing goal and a defender breathing down his neck, a ball delivered to him from the right should go to his right side and one played to him from the left would have to be directed to his left side. Harford deemed this necessary on the grounds that Shearer could look a limited player in these situations ('He doesn't really have any tricks to beat you,' he explains). His specialist knowledge on the positional habits of defenders made him believe that his passing 'rule' – which had the effect of Shearer getting the ball on the side that his marker had left 'open' – would offset this. Dalglish was less enthusiastic about the policy, arguing that Harford might be underestimating Shearer's ability and overestimating that of his adversaries.

At Blackburn, the 4–4–2 team structure that Harford implemented, a somewhat direct, no-frills style of play which was similar to that of Arsenal under George Graham, and which was geared very much to putting Shearer in positions where he could receive the ball when facing the opposing goal, led Dalglish to become anxious that the side were stereotyped.

Harford recalls that before the start of the 1994–95 season, Dalglish remarked to him that he felt that Shearer and Blackburn were too 'predictable' and he was 'bored' with the way the team were playing. 'I'm bored with it, too, Kenny,' Harford replied. 'But if we change it now, we're going to fall apart.' Harford felt that, although opponents knew what Blackburn were trying to do, having Shearer meant that they would continue to find it difficult to stop them. To his credit, Dalglish allowed Harford to have his way, and Blackburn, with Shearer revelling in having the team focused so closely on his requirements, went on to lift the title for the first time in 81 years.

As Harford points out, that Blackburn team were held up as the most shining example of 4–4–2 exponents since Everton landed the title playing that way under Howard Kendall in the mid-1980s.

When discussing Shearer's influence in making the system work so effectively for Blackburn, Harford still recalls a training session during the player's first few months at the club devoted to practising a move involving the ball being played into the space behind an opposing full-back and Shearer making a diagonal run from the middle to latch on to it. The player responsible for playing the pass was having a bad day, giving Shearer an impossible task by hitting the ball too short or too long. 'I stopped the session,' Harford says, 'but before I could say anything, Alan has shouted across to the player: "Look, you don't have to try and give the perfect ball. As long as you get it into the right sort of area, it's up to me to do something with it." Some players in Alan's position would have tried to be smart and taken the mickey, but his reaction was to take all the pressure off the fellow.'

The obvious danger of this is that it almost invited Shearer's team-mates to give him a below-par service, something which was particularly irritating to Dalglish when he saw the quality of their crosses. But Shearer, like Harford, was happy to accept a lesser standard of technical expertise; so it is little wonder that, despite all the care and attention Blackburn lavished on him, the supporting cast – the other players – were in no way resentful about their place in the scheme of things. 'The players loved him,' Harford says. 'I never heard one bad word about him from anybody.'

Shearer didn't consider himself to be someone special – in everything he did he gave the clear indication of looking upon himself as part of the team. 'He had the uncanny knack of being able to do the right thing off the field as well as on it,' Harford says. 'He could mix in any company.'

Nobody took his job more seriously than Shearer did. Yet, at the same time, he was one of the lads. When the players indulged in pranks, the seemingly whiter-than-white Shearer, whom some might have labelled Blackburn's teacher's pet, was often the instigator. 'You should talk to the coach driver,' says Harford, grinning over the memory of Shearer wheezes such as hiding the man's radio, and pelting him with cakes, oranges and water.

If Shearer's willingness to submerge himself in football's blokeish dressing-room culture was not enough to provoke the willingness of others to sacrifice some of their individuality on his behalf, the other factor was that he was the figure most liable to put win bonuses into their pockets. This is where Harford was in his element. He felt the players at his disposal were better equipped to invite opponents to come at them than they were in forcing the play themselves – and who better than Shearer, who rarely put himself into a position where colleagues had to give him the ball while he was standing still, to hit them on the break?

It seems hard to believe that he should keep causing so many headaches to Blackburn's rivals just through running on to passes through the inside-forward channels or getting on the end of crosses into the box. Harford, now West Bromwich Albion's manager, makes it seem even stranger when he says that on top of the reservations about Shearer's pace and ability on the ball, and the fact that almost all his goals are scored with his right foot, he does not even consider the player to be a particularly good athlete. 'He's a strong person rather than an athletic one,' Harford says. 'Howard Wilkinson was telling me recently that in a Newcastle training session he watched at the end of last season, they started off with a warm-up run in which Shearer and David Batty were about 40 yards behind everyone else. It was the same when Alan was at Blackburn. In pre-season cross-country runs, he was the last person you would expect to see at the front.'

This, of course, was less noticeable on the field because of Shearer's strength of character and his intelligence. No matter how closely opponents watched him, they could not do so to the extent of ignoring the ball – and it only needed their attention to be drawn to it for a split second for Shearer to escape. Equally pertinent was the time and effort devoted to developing the right sort of service to him.

To the coach, it all boiled down to 'getting Shearer turned around'. One example of this was that, in practice matches, players involved in a counter-attack had to move in the direction of the play. Harford explains: 'If the ball was knocked up to Shearer from the defence, he could not knock it back – he had to turn with it and go forward. Having played the ball up to Shearer, the only way you could get it back from him was to move forward into a position beyond him.' This was to prove of particular benefit to the striker when the matches were for real, because with one of the Blackburn midfielders bursting through on them, opposing central-defenders suddenly had another problem to deal with. 'Ian Atkins [Blackburn's midfielder] made lots of these runs beyond our front two,' Harford recalls. 'That helped Alan, if only because of the way it unsettled the defenders.'

Another aspect of Blackburn's bid to fully exploit what Shearer was good at was their work on crosses. The nature of that exercise – which lasted half an hour to an hour every day – led to some argument between Shearer and Harford. Shearer saw no reason why, when Blackburn were developing an attack down the flank, one of the wide players should not attempt to 'hit' him with the ball once they got within 25 to 30 yards of goal. Harford, again on the premise of Shearer being at his best when facing his target, preferred the crosses to be put in from more advanced positions – ideally, positions from which the ball was swinging away from the keeper and his defenders. In training, therefore, Blackburn's wide players had to get into what Harford referred to as the 'Magic Square' (the space on either side of the opposing 18-yard box) before delivering the ball into the centre; and the coach, mindful of the tendency for defenders to fall back to the edge of their six-yard box, encouraged them to to aim for what he called the 'second six-yard box' (the next six-yard area).

'Jason Wilcox [who was to establish himself in the team as an attacking left-side player] used to take the mickey out of me,' Harford recalls. 'We'd start practising the crossing and he'd suddenly put on my voice and accent and shout: "Get in the Magic Square . . . get in the Magic Square." '

It could certainly be described as a magic square for Shearer. 'Give him the right ball and you can take it for granted that he'll score,' Harford points out. 'When he doesn't, you're shocked.'

That confidence in the player was not shared by all Blackburn's fans when he joined the club. David Speedie had been their favourite player and some were so angry about his departure that a group who travelled to watch a pre-season Blackburn friendly at

SUPERMAC ON SHEARER

Of all the experts who have sat in judgement of Alan Shearer as a Newcastle centre-forward, the views of Malcolm Macdonald – or 'Supermac' as he was known among the Geordie fans who belted out the nickname to the tune of Jesus Christ Superstar – are of particular relevance. Macdonald was Shearer's predecessor in the line of outstanding No. 9s to have worn the Newcastle shirt. He joined Newcastle from Luton in May 1971, and before leaving for Arsenal five years later, bagged a total of 95 goals in 187 matches and was their top scorer four seasons in succession. He also played for England on 14 occasions – notably in the 5–0 win over Cyprus in April 1975, when he put himself in the record books by scoring all five goals.

Macdonald was not a 'born' goalscorer; he started his career as a left-back and his transformation into a centre-forward owed much to his ability to analyse the technical requirements of the role and how he could get the best out of himself in it. This is one of the characteristics which leads Macdonald to say that he can see part of himself in Shearer. He points out that, as in his case, Shearer's success has been due to the way he has applied himself rather than to natural ability. There are also similarities between their styles of play. Macdonald feels that, though he had greater pace than Shearer and was superior in the air, Shearer has the edge in ball-playing ability. Nonetheless, if you see recordings of Macdonald in action – particularly when he was chasing balls through the inside-forward channels – you could easily mistake him for Shearer.

The biggest difference between them, perhaps, lies in their personalities and the extent of the control they exert over themselves. Macdonald is the more headstrong and individualistic of the two – an all-or-nothing person who, as a player and then a manager (with Fulham), exuded a self-confidence that occasionally seemed to border on arrogance. Today, nothing can be more educational than a conversation with him on Britain's leading goalscorers – Shearer especially.

Macdonald has always believed in strikers needing to be 'selfish' to get the most out of themselves as scorers. He considers this to be the main area where Shearer differs from him. He recalls that one of the first people he met after signing for Newcastle was the great Jackie Milburn, the club's highly acclaimed England centre-forward of the 1950s. 'I've never forgotten that meeting,' Macdonald says. 'We were talking about the pressures of wearing the Newcastle No. 9 shirt and he told me: "You have to make friends with the crowd, and all you have to do to do that is score goals. You have to make sure that you are just as capable of scoring a goal in the last minute as you are in the first minute."'

Macdonald's interpretation of the advice led to some friction with his Newcastle coaches and managers who felt that he did not involve himself enough in Newcastle's play outside the box, not to mention the team-mates who might just as well have said goodbye to the ball if Macdonald had it in what he perceived as a potential scoring position. His attitude was best summed up by a brush with Don Howe when Howe was his coach at Arsenal. Howe had set up an training session to work on moves to create chances for players other than the recognised strikers, one aspect of which involved Macdonald making runs to the flanks to create space in the middle for team-mates moving up from deep positions and getting the ball in to them.

Macdonald, true to his rebellious nature in these circumstances, asked: 'Why do

I have to knock the ball into a midfield player or a defender? What's he going to do with it?'

'Well, he's got a goal chance,' Howe explained.

'That can't be right,' Macdonald argued. 'Why do you want me out here when I can score goals, and someone else in there when he can't score goals?'

'Don't complicate it,' Howe snapped.

'I'm not complicating it,' Macdonald told him. 'If anything, I'm simplifying it. What ball am I going to knock in?' he persisted. 'The kind of ball I like to receive will be no good to the player in the middle because he won't know what to do with it, whereas if he's out on the flank, he can knock in any ball he likes and I will get on the end of it.'

And so it went on, with Howe inevitably becoming more and more exasperated. This is not the sort of training-ground scene you can imagine ever being created by Shearer, which is good news for opposing defenders as far as Macdonald is concerned. As he says: 'Can you imagine how many more goals he would get if he had my attitude?'

Still, if anybody has got the balance between goalscoring and general team-play right, it is Shearer. Indeed, as a goal machine, he strikes Macdonald as being in the same class as any of the strikers he has ever seen.

Here's how Macdonald describes some of the Shearer goals that have put him in that category:

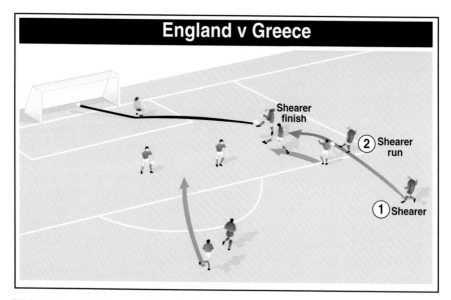

England v Greece

ENGLAND v GREECE, 17 May 1994

England 5 (Anderton, Beardsley, Platt 2, Shearer) Greece 0

How's this for a positive attitude and power finish? Shearer has been able to get a run at the Greek central defender, and when he is gathering momentum there's no way that he's going to be stopped from attacking the space. Shearer's shot was so close to the keeper it might well have seemed that it lacked accuracy. In fact, the reverse was true. The closer you strike the ball to a keeper's feet – and especially when you hit it as hard as Shearer does – the harder it is for him to get down to it.

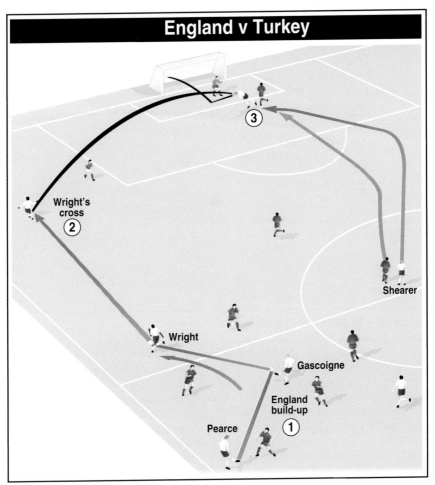

England v Turkey

Wright's cross ②

Wright

Shearer

Gascoigne

England build-up ①

Pearce

③

ENGLAND v TURKEY, 18 November 1992

England 4 (Gascoigne 2, Shearer, Pearce) Turkey 0

This goal bore the hallmark of a genuine scorer, in that Shearer was not interested in getting involved in the build-up play; all he was concerned with was finding a position from which he could get on the end of it. His run initially took him and the defender marking him away from the ball. This is an important part of the art of scoring goals – you drag defenders away from certain areas to give yourself the scope to suddenly come back into them. When a striker makes a run off the ball, it is nearly always a curved run, as opposed to a straight one. The curve of Shearer's run on this occasion had the effect of increasing his angle of vision and giving him time to plan his next move. A defender only needs to take his eyes off Shearer for a split second – something which he has to do to check the overall picture – for Shearer to lose him. His run on this occasion made it particularly difficult for the defender. He took off like an express train when he could see Ian Wright poised to knock the ball into the middle, and the timing of the run was such that the defender really could do nothing about it.

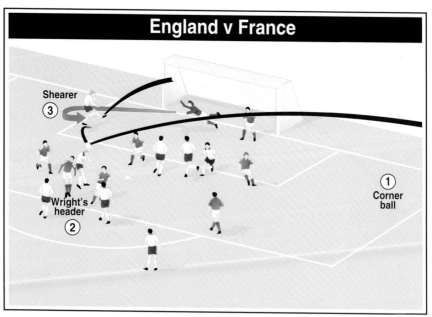

England v France

ENGLAND v FRANCE, 19 February 1992

England 2 (Shearer, Lineker) France 0

This was Shearer's England début, and even before the goal he was giving the French problems with his movement and doggedness. The French were not good at defending corners and free-kicks and the goal was an example of this – they should have had someone on the back post. But you have to give Shearer credit for knowing where the space was and for hiding this from the opposition by not going into it too early. When the corner was taken he was standing almost on the goal-line, virtually on the keeper's toes, and the main danger appeared to be posed by the three England players on the edge of their six-yard box. Suddenly, Shearer pulled off backwards, into that vacant space, and when the ball broke to him from Mark Wright's header, the speed with which he spun on it and got in the shot was tremendous.

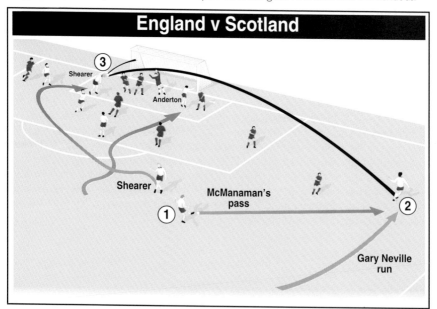

England v Scotland

ENGLAND v SWITZERLAND, 8 June 1996

England 1 (Shearer) Switzerland 1

It is often said that goalkeepers should not be beaten by near-post shots, but the power behind Shearer's strikes make them an exception. For once, he has joined in the build-up play, coming off the centre-half to take a pass from Gascoigne and lay it off to Ince. Then, he's off looking for a finishing position. As Ince comes forward with the ball, Shearer has to suddenly check to avoid running into an offside position – a manoeuvre which affects the concentration of the player marking him, and also gives Shearer an angle of view where he can see both Ince and the defender. His marker turns his attention to Ince – and it is at this precise moment, with the Swiss struggling to react to the pace and movement of the England attack, that Ince releases the ball into the space behind them for Shearer to do his stuff. Superb timing on the part of Ince and Shearer.

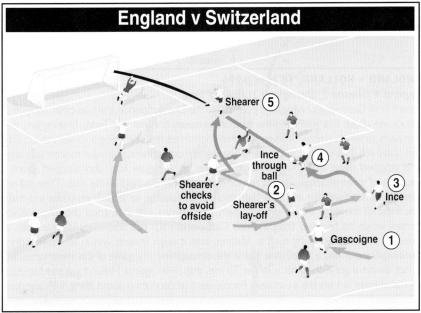

ENGLAND v SCOTLAND, 15 June 1996

England 2 (Shearer, Gascoigne) Scotland 0

A brilliant cross from Gary Neville, but look at the run Shearer has made and the way he has outwitted the whole Scotland defence. The hardest run in football to cover is the one that goes away from the ball, as Shearer shows here. He has gone as far away from the ball as he can and is running across their defenders towards the other side of the field. They are obviously finding it difficult to watch both the ball and the player at the same time and are much more concerned with the England players closer to the ball. In that respect, Shearer was helped by a great run by Darren Anderton to the near post. It caught the defender who had come forward to confront him in two minds, and prompted the defender to go with Anderton. The Scotland defenders were 'sucked in' towards the near post, the goalkeeper was half-covering that area, and I think they were all taken by surprise by the quality of Neville's cross. It looked easy for Shearer, didn't it? He just seemed to be 'lucky' in being in the right place at the right time. It wasn't luck – it was intelligence and anticipation.

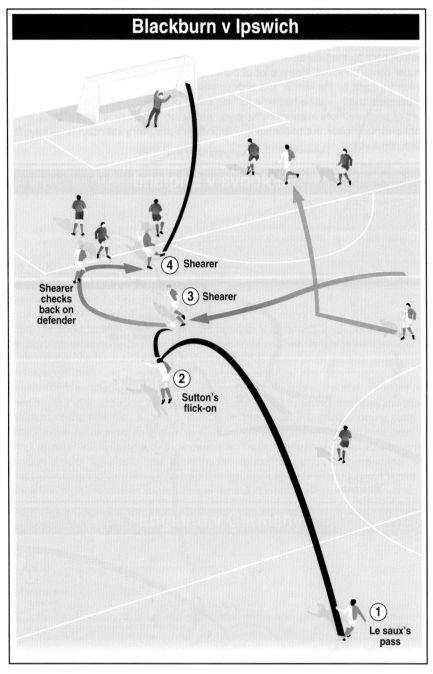

Blackburn v Ipswich

① Le saux's pass

② Sutton's flick-on

③ Shearer

④ Shearer

Shearer checks back on defender

BLACKBURN v IPSWICH, 28 January 1995

Blackburn 4 (Shearer 3, Sherwood) Ipswich 1

Little wonder that Blackburn won the Championship that season. Shearer has come from an isolated position to latch onto Sutton's flick-on and his obvious route to goal is through the inside-left/outside-left channel. But he has suddenly checked back on the defender tracking him, gets the ball onto that right foot, and curls it into the far corner of the net. Everyone is left gobsmacked. Magic.

Darlington (one of Speedie's former clubs) unfurled a banner which read: 'Speedie in, Shearer out.' But it was not long before this message was made to look somewhat misguided. In Blackburn's first Premiership match of the 1992–93 season at Crystal Palace, Shearer marked his league début with two thrilling goals in a 3–3 draw.

His striking partner was Mike Newell, and the rest of Blackburn's starting line-up comprised Bobby Mimms in goal, David May, Colin Hendry, Kevin Moran and Alan Wright at the back, and Stuart Ripley, Tim Sherwood, Mark Atkins and Tony Dobson in midfield. In view of his renowned ability to handle pressure, who could have been surprised that it was very much Shearer's day?

In addition to his own goals, he had a hand in Blackburn's other strike – by Newell – and set up two other chances with crosses (both cut back from the goal-line) that any winger would have been proud to produce. He himself had his first scoring opportunities in the opening 15 minutes, taking a Ripley cross but failing to control the ball well enough to get in a shot, and then producing a strike which was deflected away from the target by a Palace defender's legs. But trust Shearer to keep going – and to produce something truly special.

It came midway through the second half, just after Palace had taken a 2–1 lead. They had no reason to suspect that they would not hold it when Shearer collected a ball on his chest some 25 yards from goal. Yet as the ball dropped and opponents were moving in to take it off him, he blasted an extraordinary right-foot volley into the net. 'It was like Roy of the Rovers – absolutely unbelievable,' Harford recalls. 'It's on one of his videos; and when I look at it now, the thing I enjoy about it the most is the sight of Newelly running down the pitch, going bananas over it. At the time, I just thought about what Alan was capable of doing for our side. I thought: "Here we go."'

Shearer must have been reading his mind. Near the end, he burst through the Palace defence from the halfway line and beat the keeper with another shot from outside the box.

Later, Palace's manager Steve Coppell, whose team had salvaged a point with a Gareth Southgate goal in the last minute, attempted to instil a sense of perspective into the acclaim for Shearer's performance. He could hardly disagree that Shearer and Newell looked as good a partnership as any ('They are both very mobile players and their potential together is obviously immense') but he added: 'If you take Shearer's scoring record over the last 100 games, then it's not a prolific one. He can't rely on scoring the type of goals he got today every week. His manager will be looking for returns from inside the six-yard box as well. That is where a striker proves himself.'

Shearer did not make too much of his achievement either: 'I couldn't have dreamed or hoped to score two like that.' He was asked the obvious question of how he felt with such a big price tag on his shoulders. 'Personally, I wouldn't pay that for me,' was his response.

By the turn of the year, however, his goals total was beginning to make him look a bargain. Following his Palace début, he had gone on to get 14 more goals (including three penalties) in the next 20 Premiership matches to push Blackburn into a strong position for the title, and six in their opening four Coca-Cola Cup ties. One team who suffered more than most at the boots of Shearer were Norwich. On 3 October, in Blackburn's 11th Premiership match, they were thrashed 7–1 at Ewood Park – a result that took Blackburn to the top of the table – and Shearer scored twice. One reason why Harford still remembers it particularly is that both Shearer goals came from long passes out of defence by Colin Hendry. 'The Charlie Ball,' he explains. 'People did not say we were predictable in that game, but we were.'

Shearer himself was predictable again when the two teams met in the Coca-Cola Cup third round at Blackburn on 28 October, firing in the first goal in a 2–0 win direct from a quickly taken free-kick.

Harford was not alone in singing the striker's praises. Anyone who was anyone in football did so, too, and with Blackburn and Manchester United at the top of the table, one man who found himself in particular demand for his views on the subject was Shearer's team-mate Kevin Moran, a former United player. Was Alex Ferguson's failure to land Shearer going to rebound on him? 'It's hard for me to say they [United] have blown it,' Moran said. 'I still have a lot of friends at the old place [Old Trafford]. But what I will say is that I already regard Shearer as a real snip at the price Blackburn paid for him, and you haven't seen the best of him yet. He is still only learning. He reminds me of a younger version of Mark Hughes. Quicker than Sparky, but with the same sharpness, power of shot and ability to give any defender a real hard time physically. He has fantastic awareness, too. All I can say to United is that I would rather play with him than against him.'

By the turn of the year, Blackburn looked a good bet to win at least one trophy. But, with Shearer sustaining the right knee cruciate ligament injury which put him out of their team for the second half of the season – and threatened his whole career – they faltered in the Championship (they finished fourth behind Manchester United, Aston Villa and Norwich), the Coca-Cola Cup (they lost in the semi-final to Sheffield Wednesday), and the FA Cup (they fell to Sheffield United in the sixth round).

In a season in which England had begun their qualifying campaign for the 1994 World Cup finals, in a group which also contained Norway, Poland, Holland, Turkey and San Marino, his injury hardly came at a good time for the national team either.

In his opening international match of the season, on 9 September, England were beaten 1–0 by Spain in Santander, and Shearer, who operated virtually on his own in the middle with England's other forwards, David White and Nigel Clough, foraging in deep positions, was subjected to what he described as the worst physical battering of his career. 'I couldn't believe what was going on,' he said. 'I can remember only two occasions when I got the ball and they didn't foul me. Every other time it came to me, I finished on the floor. I played for the Under-21s two years ago when the

Mexicans had three players sent off against us but this was totally different. The Mexicans were niggling and spitting. They were not making the sort of physical contact I had to deal with against Spain.'

The pain, though, was eased by Graham Taylor's praise for his resilience. 'I thought his performance was one of the good things to come out of the game for us,' he said. 'Some players at this level like Shearer take it in their stride, blossom and are positive, while others crumble. What we must do is get more support up there for him.'

Three days later, when Blackburn beat Arsenal 1–0 at Highbury (with a goal from Mike Newell), Shearer was in the wars again. He ended up needing four stitches in his lip and three more above his eye – both, he claimed, the result of challenges involving Tony Adams. 'I got the same sort of treatment playing for England in Spain,' Shearer said. 'But this time I've got more cuts.' While explaining that the lip injury was caused by Adams catching him with his elbow, he refused to make a song and dance about it. Instead, he made a joke. His wife was due to give birth to their first child – Chloe – the following week, and he quipped: 'My biggest worry is that my wife won't let me in the labour ward looking like this. She won't recognise me.'

In his private moments, however, such experiences are bound to have had a considerable influence on him. Over the years, he has acquired the reputation of being a centre-forward who knows how to look after himself, a player liable occasionally to give out as much 'stick' as he takes. He never was a striker who could be easily intimidated, but those matches against Spain and Arsenal might well have been a turning point for him in deciding how much his physical approach to the game needed to be developed.

In the meantime, his character underwent a test of a different kind, first in England's opening World Cup qualifying match against Norway – then top of the group with maximum points from three games – at Wembley on 14 October. Shearer must have been encouraged that Taylor, true to his word to give him greater support up front, chose Arsenal's Ian Wright to be his partner for the first time. He did seem to have slight worries that the England team did not have a natural wide player to stretch the Norwegian defence, but said: 'It will be up to the four midfielders and Ian and myself to provide a bit of width. I'm feeling confident, so hopefully we can get a couple of goals between us to get us off to a good start.'

England, though, could only manage one, thanks to David Platt, and it was not enough; Norway came from behind to hold them to a 1–1 draw. That meant that England had scored only five goals in seven internationals (all of them coming from Platt) – and more pressure was placed on Shearer for the next qualifying match, against Turkey at Wembley on 18 November. An extra burden for him was that he had gone four successive Premiership matches without scoring, a spell in which no other Blackburn player was able to find the net either, and Rovers dropped from first to second in the table.

Publicly, his reaction to this hardly gave the impression of a striker fast approaching the point where he was going to become a suitable case for treatment. 'If you let it get to you, you end up trying too hard and that affects your performance,' Shearer said. 'All I can do is go out and carry on as I was playing before. All it needs is one little tap-in and you're back on the goal trail.'

A little tap-in? After Paul Gascoigne had given England an early lead, Shearer gave them more leeway to relax by applying the finishing touch to a great build-up (and especially a great Ian Wright cross) with a diving header. It was his third goal in six England matches, and in his next six matches for Blackburn, he added another four, including two in the 3–1 defeat of Leeds on Boxing Day, to help keep them in second place and consolidate his position as the Premiership's leading scorer.

It was then that Shearer, the young man who seemed to love seeing obstacles barring his path, suffered the biggest setback of his career. He had to go off against Leeds after injuring his right knee – the one on which he had undergone a cartilage operation two years earlier – while stretching for a shot in an attempt to clinch a hat-trick. It did not look a serious problem; even when he lasted only 30 minutes of Blackburn's Coca-Cola Cup fourth-round tie at Cambridge on 6 January, his comeback game after missing their two Premiership matches, there was no real indication of the anxiety that would follow for him. An examination revealed a slight tear in the cartilage, necessitating a minor 'keyhole' surgery operation on 11 January. A month later, though, when Shearer can have been expected to be ready to return to action, the knee was still troubling him. It prompted him to make a return visit to Cambridge, this time to see Professor David Dandy, a surgeon renowned in professional football for his expertise in dealing with such injuries; and he was confronted with the worst news he could have had.

It was discovered that he had torn his anterior cruciate ligament (which runs diagonally through the knee joint and controls its movement). Shearer's efforts to come to terms with this can't have been helped by the horror stories concerning other top players who had suffered this fate. Paul Gascoigne, who sustained a similar injury in making that infamous tackle on Nottingham Forest's Gary Charles in the 1991 FA Cup final, was out of action for more than a year (although in his case, his problems were compounded by a broken knee-cap). West Ham's Julian Dicks suffered even more torment – he was out for 16 months.

The gloom that descended on Shearer can only have deepened in the ensuing months. Quite apart from Blackburn's slide without him – they won no more than half of the 21 Premiership matches he missed – he was also on the outside looking in for England's World Cup qualifying matches against San Marino (h 6–0), Turkey (a 2–0), Holland (h 2–2), Poland (a 1–1), Norway (a 0–2), and the prestige friendlies against Germany, Brazil and the United States in America in the summer. His unavailability enabled other Premiership strikers, notably Les Ferdinand and Teddy Sheringham, to stake their claims in the side.

Still, in his bid to get over the injury quickly and return to the

Premiership as effective as ever, Shearer certainly went to the right person for his operation. Dandy, who had been specialising in knee surgery for more than 20 years, was noted for what he called his 'heavy duty' repair job – that of placing strips of tissue through the centre of the knee joint and around it. The other thing which helped Shearer, of course, was his strength of character.

Within eight months, he was back playing again – and bursting to make up for lost time. By the start of the 1993–94 season, his recovery was sufficiently advanced for Blackburn to put him in a substitute role for their pre-season matches. Harford recalls: 'We were playing a game in Ireland, and 15 minutes from the end Kenny says to him: "Get warmed up." It frightened the life out of me because Alan had not played for eight months and I wasn't sure that we weren't rushing things unnecessarily. I'm saying: "For God's sake, Kenny, don't put him on – he ain't ready." As it turned out, Kenny did put him on and Alan scored two goals in about five minutes. But when the season started, Kenny went the other way and put the reins on him. He was on the subs bench for the opening games and it was not until the ninth game of the season that Alan got into the starting line-up.

'I think Kenny was trying to make the point to him that he had not proved he was ready for Premiership football again just because he'd scored a couple of goals in a pre-season friendly. It was difficult because, when you were sitting with him on the bench, he could drive you potty. He'd nag you non-stop – "Get me on, get me on" – and you'd literally have to tell him to shut up.'

On the basis of actions speaking louder than words, Shearer produced an appropriate retort on 29 August, when he was brought on at Newcastle after 67 minutes and scored the goal – from Tim Sherwood's through-pass 15 minutes from the end – which gave Blackburn a 1–1 draw. In his first full appearance of the season, on 25 September, he was again on the mark in a 1–1 draw at home to Sheffield Wednesday.

At this stage, Shearer conceded that the muscles and hamstring supporting the knee still needed strengthening, but added: 'I'm not feeling it [the knee] at all. I am certainly not going to be pulling out of any tackles and anything like that. If I start doing that, I lose a lot. The physical side is an important part of my game and, if I start to become less committed, I will go downhill as a player. If anything, I am going to the other extreme just to prove that I am all right.'

In that season, Blackburn improved their Championship position by two places – they finished runners-up to Manchester United – and Shearer ended up with 31 goals (including one penalty) in 40 Premiership matches. On the international front, too, he was back in business, albeit without being able to achieve the success he yearned for. Left out of the first World Cup qualifying tie of the season, against Poland at Wembley (a 3–0 England win on 8 September), he made his international comeback in the crucial penultimate qualifying clash with Holland in Rotterdam on 13 October.

With the top two teams in the group guaranteed a place in the 1994 finals in the United States, England and Holland were joint second, behind Norway, and Holland had the slight edge on goal difference. Taylor's confidence in England getting a win or a draw in Rotterdam was boosted further by the knowledge that Shearer was now fit enough to return to the side. Taylor saw this for himself on 2 October, when he watched Shearer demoralise newly promoted Swindon with two goals and a hand in the other in a 3–1 Blackburn win; three days later, his assistant, Lawrie McMenemy, also waxed lyrical about the player's fitness after seeing him in a Coca-Cola Cup tie in atrocious conditions at Bournemouth.

Shearer lined up against the Dutch alongside Paul Merson. But for him and everyone involved with the England team, the big night produced only agony, as the opposition romped to a 2–0 win. The only route to the finals now open to England was the highly improbable one of their winning a landslide in San Marino on 27 November, and Holland losing in Poland on the same night. England, with Shearer missing from the line-up because of a back injury, won 7–1, with Ian Wright leading the rout with five and

Paul Ince and Les Ferdinand adding the others. Meanwhile, though, Dennis Bergkamp was inspiring a 3–1 Dutch win in Poznan to render England's performance meaningless and leave us talking more about the goal England conceded – only San Marino's second in the whole competition – than about Wright's achievement in equalling the England scoring record established by Malcolm Macdonald against Cyprus in 1975.

All of which left the much-maligned Graham Taylor at the end of his Football Association contract – and his England bosses scratching their heads on the question of who might be able to do a better job. Few fans felt they had picked the wrong man to succeed Taylor when they appointed Terry Venables, arguably the most innovative, imaginative coach in British football, to replace him.

But Venables' methods did create problems for Shearer. England, the host nation for the 1996 European Championship finals and therefore spared the qualifying battle, had only friendly matches to look forward to throughout the two years leading up to the competition – and, having been excluded from the World Cup party in the United States, Venables took the opportunity to start experimenting early.

The first idea that was put into operation concerned giving England what Venables described as a 'Christmas Tree' formation, a 4–5–1 system in which Shearer took on a 'Lone Ranger' role up front. On the face of it, this did seem to work quite well, especially as the men who were immediately behind Shearer – and who were expected to push forward in support of him – were players of the calibre of Paul Gascoigne, David Platt, Peter Beardsley and Darren Anderton.

In England's first match under Venables, against Denmark at Wembley on 9 March, Platt scored the only goal. The strategy looked even more impressive in the next match, against Greece on 17 May, when England won 5–0 with goals from Shearer, Platt (two), Anderton and Beardsley. In both matches, however, it had been noticeable that Shearer had found scoring chances for himself difficult to come by and that Beardsley, a master of the art of bringing the best out of fellow forwards, seemed to spend much of his time isolated from Shearer on the left flank.

Venables denied that Shearer was unhappy with the system, revealing that when he had asked him for an opinion on how it was going for him, the striker had replied: 'Terrific.' Venables added: 'Platt and Beardsley are essentially functioning as forwards. So Shearer is not left isolated in the opposition area any more than Ian Rush was for Liverpool when they were at their most effective or than he is himself with Blackburn. Obviously, it is a great advantage for attackers to come into the box from deeper positions because they arrive facing the goal, which creates more options for them and for the man who is already there.'

Shearer could have had no arguments against that in principle. In practice, though, it was a different matter. England's next match of the season was a dull 0–0 draw at home to Norway on 22 May. As far as England were concerned, things were to get worse for Shearer before they got better in Euro 96. Though he scored both goals in the 2–0 win over the United States at the start of the 1994–95 season, he then hit a drought which was to last for 21 months. In that 1994–95 season, the teams against whom he couldn't score were Romania, Nigeria, Japan, Sweden and Brazil. As if to reinforce the view that Shearer might not be as good an international player as we thought he was, even the little-known Norwegian part-timers of Trelleborg, shock winners over Blackburn in the first round of the UEFA Cup, only conceded one Shearer goal in two matches.

The achievement of subduing Shearer, however, was a distinction that continued to be denied to the vast majority of the sides who had to oppose him in the Premiership. It was as if they caught the backlash of his England problems, because he scored his highest number of Blackburn goals – 34, including ten penalties – in 42 matches, and he at last got his hands on a Championship-winners' medal, the honour he most coveted.

Manchester United, who finished runners-up, couldn't say they hadn't been warned. One of their very few hiccups on the way to beating Blackburn to the title in 1994 had been a 2–0 defeat at Ewood Park in April, which cut the gap between the two teams to three points with seven matches left. Shearer got both goals, in the 46th and 76th minutes, and Patrick Barclay, in his report of the match for *The Observer*, described them particularly lucidly when he wrote: 'The second half had hardly begun when Blackburn went for it, and got it. Neat play on the right involving Batty and Newell took the ball to Sherwood, who chipped it forward for Shearer. With a yard or two of space around the penalty spot, the England centre-forward was in his element. He steadied himself and drove across Schmeichel with fearsome power . . . United were finally quelled when Shearer broke free to demonstrate to the citizens of his adopted home that Walker could have bought no more accomplished a spearhead for the club's drive to the big-time, nor one with a greater capacity for producing heroic deeds when they are most required.'

CHAPTER EIGHT

Striking Partners

One of Alan Shearer's most laudable characteristics is his willingness to try to adjust to different team-mates and playing systems. Mike Newell, his former Blackburn striking partner, puts it this way: 'If he were a prima donna, he would say: "I'm Alan Shearer – I've scored X-amount of goals and that formation or that player is no good to me." But he's not like that. If he isn't entirely happy or comfortable about something, he is strong enough to make people aware of it. But that does not mean he won't go through with it, and give 100 per cent.'

Shearer was confronted with such a situation for the 1994–95 season when Blackburn signed Chris Sutton from Norwich for £5 million. In a number of ways, the purchase of Sutton, a centre-forward who could also play at centre-half, was good news for Shearer. It relieved him of the burden of being Britain's costliest player, and Newell and his other striking partner, Kevin Gallacher, were both out of action through injury. Things got even better in Blackburn's matches, with the combination of Shearer and Sutton – the so-called 'SAS' team – steering the club to the Championship. Between them, the pair accounted for 49 of the club's 80 Premiership goals, with Shearer registering the highest total of his career – before or since – with 34. It was the first time that a player had scored more than 30 goals in consecutive seasons in the top flight since Jimmy Greaves managed the feat in the 1960s, and in addition to his Championship-winners' medal, Shearer also gained the personal reward of being voted the Professional Footballers Association player of the year.

The irony of all this is that if Shearer had been able to choose his own partner for that season, he would probably have plumped for Newell rather than Sutton. The two men were the closest of friends off the field, and on it they had established a rapport similar to the one that Shearer would later experience with Teddy Sheringham in the England team.

Of all the players who have worked with Shearer as a senior professional, Newell is arguably the one who has got to know him best. Five years older than Shearer, and possessing a beanpole build – 6ft 1ins and 11 stone – that tended to make him look ungainly, Newell had arrived at Blackburn in November 1991, via spells with Liverpool (his home-city club), Crewe, Wigan, Luton (where he worked with Ray Harford) and Everton. He was the first striker that Kenny Dalglish bought for Blackburn, something of a proud distinction for Newell because Dalglish was his idol; and, appropriately, it was Newell who clinched Blackburn's promotion to the Premiership with the penalty goal that gave them their 1–0 win over Leicester in the 1992 play-off final.

Newell could easily have followed this by taking Shearer's place at Southampton. In Blackburn's negotiations with the Saints for the England striker, Ian Branfoot singled out Newell as his top choice among the group of Ewood Park players he considered taking as a part-exchange deal. Blackburn countered this with the high valuation figure they put on the player so Southampton, anxious to get the most from the deal in terms of hard cash, settled for the lower-priced David Speedie instead.

Though Newell's scoring record was far from impressive, it was not difficult to see why Branfoot was attracted to him and, indeed, why Blackburn and Shearer were grateful for his continued presence at the club. He was an intelligent, exceptionally hard-working player who liked nothing better than to involve himself in the build-up play and create scoring chances for others. This, he recalls, had been a habit ever since his brief spell on Liverpool's books as a junior. He recalls: 'I used to play in midfield – it wasn't until I was 17 or 18 that I became a striker – and really I played all over the pitch in those days. Even as a striker, I have never been one to just stand there waiting for the ball to come to me. I know this might sound stupid, but I get just as much enjoyment from heading the ball off my own goal-line as I do in heading it into the net at the other end.

'I think I have always had that enthusiasm, and the other thing is that I'm a naturally fit person. I have never carried any excess weight at all, and have been able to run and run all day. I used to take it to the extreme; coaches used to say to me: "It's great that you're giving people passing options, but you don't always need to be flying about all over the place." It was probably only when I got to Blackburn – when I was in my mid-20s and starting to reach my peak – that I learnt to control this aspect of my game.'

Fortunately for Shearer, though, even a more subdued Newell was liable to cover more ground in a match, and do more to help his striking partner, than most other players.

Blackburn were on a pre-season tour of Scotland when Shearer was signed, and Newell recalls: 'He just arrived at our hotel one morning, when we were due to play our last game against Hibernian, and straightaway we got on like a house on fire. Initially, it didn't happen for us on the field – I didn't play against Hibernian, and even with Alan in the side, Hibs beat us 3–0. This was probably what you would have expected because they were a couple of weeks ahead of us in their training, but you could almost see Alan thinking: "Oh, what have I done?" When I got to know him better, I remember him saying to me that on the journey home from the trip he was wondering if signing for Blackburn had been a mistake. But Blackburn then went to play a couple of matches in Ireland, and in the first game against Drogheda [when Shearer was brought on as a substitute to partner Newell in the second half], we were fortunate enough to hit it off immediately. I know we weren't playing a particularly good team – we won by five or six – but, honestly, we just seemed to be telepathic. It was the same off the field. We had been put in a room together – not out of choice, it was just the way someone had done the room list – and we got on so well, it was as if we were brothers.'

Newell suggests this might have been partly because, in addition to sharing the same basic views about football, they were both committed family men who had been brought up with similar moral and ethical values. They were both strong-minded characters, too. So they had a perfect understanding of where each other was coming from, and the longer they worked together, the stronger the bond between them became.

That bond, which extended to their families, was initially developed during Shearer's first few weeks as a Blackburn player when he was living in a local hotel and spending the occasional evening having dinner and watching football on TV at Newell's home. 'He just made himself at home,' Newell recalls. 'He was never shy – that's the thing I remember most about him then. If he wanted more food, he would ask for more food. You know, he was so straightforward and honest. There was no "side" to him – you knew he was a person you could trust.'

Not long afterwards, Shearer moved into a rented house in Southport, and he and Newell – who lived near by in Formby – started travelling to training together each day. Six months later, Shearer bought a house in the same street as Newell.

The fact that the two players were so close did not mean that they had the same temperament and personality or that they did not clash occasionally. Off the field, Newell, the more talented of the two academically – he left school with seven O-levels – could be as aggressive and argumentative as Shearer was laid-back and philosophical. Football arguments were liable to become somewhat animated, if not fiery, when Newell was involved. Such was Newell's apparently stroppy manner, in fact, that he was nicknamed 'Mr Angry'.

'I just voice my opinions,' he says. 'I do like an argument, and I can argue with someone for hours and hours yet get up the next morning having forgotten about it. Even if it gets heated – a bit personal – I don't fall out with anybody.' It was the same, he says, in his clashes with Shearer, 'Well, it's like husband and wife, isn't it?'

One of the most common reasons for their disputes was Shearer's anxiety about being late for training. Shearer, who took it upon himself to drive goalkeeper Tim Flowers to the ground as well as Newell, would often arrive at Newell's house – his last pick-up point – earlier than anticipated. 'He could get quite agitated if I was not ready to leave immediately,' Newell recalls. 'I'd just be finishing my Weetabix or whatever, and he'd be virtually stamping his feet and telling me it was "ignorant" to be late. "No, it's not ignorant," I'd tell him. "Sometimes, it's ignorant to be early." The point was, it didn't matter if we left ten minutes before he said he would be at my place, or ten minutes after – there was no way we were ever going to be late for training.'

That 50-minute journey was often the highlight of Newell's day. 'The time flashed past because the chat between the three of us was so good. Alan, myself and Tim, we had a great time. People who only know Alan from what they see of him on TV don't realise what good company he is. He is very much one of the lads – he likes to have a laugh and a joke just as much as everybody else. He's very sharp, very bright.'

He also had a way of bringing out that argumentative streak in Newell. 'If we were talking about other players, and I was praising someone, he would wind me up by saying: "Oh, he's a crap player, him." He would get me going over daft things. I remember that one day we passed a new car, and the lads were asking what make it was. Alan said it was a Toyota, and I said it was a Honda. He said: "It was a Toyota, Michael," and I said: "No way, Alan, it was a Honda." He actually had me going for five minutes, and I was getting so uptight that the roof was coming off the car. To prove it was a Honda, I even slowed down to let the car pass us, and it was then that I caught sight of Tim in the mirror, almost in tears with laughter.

'Sometimes, I'd have a go at him over things he said on TV,' Newell recalls. 'When he was being interviewed about his part in

Blackburn's success, he would say: "It's all about what Blackburn do, not what Alan Shearer does." He had a habit of talking about himself in the third person, and I would imitate him as a sort of piss-take. But, for some reason, I did find it a bit irritating. I used to say to him: "Why do you keep saying your name? Everyone knows who you are."'

The differences between them as people – in their everyday habits – were particularly apparent when they were room-mates on away trips. 'The thing about Alan is that he is a very methodical person, much more so than I am,' Newell explains. 'When we were away, he would make a point of ringing certain people – like his parents and Jack Hixon – every day. "What's the crack?" he'd ask. Even if he hadn't got anything to tell them and he knew they had nothing to tell him, he would still ring. It was like a ritual, something he needed to do to be able to feel relaxed and comfortable.

'He's the sort of person who needs to do the same things, follow the same routine, day in, day out. Methodical – yes, that's a good word for him. As soon as we got to our hotel room, he would start unpacking straightaway – his suit would immediately be taken out of its carrier, with the jacket being hung up in the wardrobe and the trousers put in the trouser press; his two toiletry bags would be placed in the bathroom, and so on. The first things I would do would be to throw my bag on the floor, hang the suit-carrier up in the wardrobe and get on the bed.

'In the mornings, he is the liveliest person you could ever meet. It takes me a bit of time to get myself together, whereas Alan – at eight o'clock in the morning – is as regular as clockwork. You knew he would get the papers from under the door, switch the bedside light on, put the TV on, open the curtains, and say: "Good morning, Michael." The bedside light was the thing that annoyed me. I'd say: "Look, I don't mind you opening the curtains to let the light in, but is it necessary to have the light on as well?" As I said, he has a routine that he has to get into.'

But Newell had no complaints about Shearer's routine on the

field. 'We could both play, but the big thing was that we knew our strengths. I knew that if I had the ball on the right and he was at the back post, all I needed to do was take one touch and whip it short because Alan was brilliant at getting on the shoulder of a defender and then running across him at the last moment. It was the same when he was running towards the penalty spot – all I had to do was drop the ball over the centre-half's head. Basically, he knew that if I had the ball, and he was in a better position than me, then he would get it – there was no way that I was going to try and do something clever. It was the same with him.

'When Blackburn started in the Premiership, we had a big, solid back four, and four strung across the middle of the field, and a lot of the matches were real physical battles. If we were in trouble away from home – and even *at* home – the ball would be knocked forward long and it would be up to Alan and me to make something of it. It was a good way of turning teams around, and once we had got them turned around, we could start playing our football. Whether it was a long ball from the full-back, or a goal-kick, Alan and I were always in close contact, with one of us going for the ball and the other supporting him. I mean, you can play with some players who might be 20 or 30 yards away from you, and all you can do is help the ball along. But this did not happen with Alan and me. We looked upon ourselves as a team within a team.'

With Shearer and Newell up front, Blackburn were able to become one of the most effective counter-attacking teams in the country. Before long, opposing sides, wary about pushing forward to the extent of leaving too much space behind them, started to drop back – but this made little difference to Rovers' strikers. In fact, it was in this situation that Newell's willingness to forage in deeper areas – to be what Ray Harford describes as a 'half-centre-forward' as opposed to a 'full' one – was of the greatest help to his striking colleague.

'Centre-halves love to have someone to mark,' Newell explains, 'and with Alan right up there, and me dropping off him into a deeper position, they had problems straightaway. They were so scared of Alan that, instead of one of the two central-defenders pushing forward onto me, they would both stay in there. At times I couldn't believe the space I was getting, and it was great for Alan, too, because it can be easier to create space for yourself when it's one against two than when there are two of you up front and you're being marked man for man.

'Ray Harford was very keen on my playing behind Alan, because when we were defending it gave us another man who could pinch the ball, and when the attack broke down it was amazing the number of times the ball just happened to break into my area. I could have the ball played into me, and turn with it, and that's when the two central-defenders were in trouble because Alan would just make a run off them and you could put it in for him.'

Ray Harford says: 'I always felt that someone like Newell, or Paul Kitson [who played with Shearer in the England Under-21 team] would be better with Alan than a player like Chris Sutton. Mickey was happier to make a goal than score a goal, especially for somebody like Shearer who was his bosom pal, but Sutton was not like that. I'm not saying Chris did not make chances for Alan – he did – but the problem was that both players were No. 9s, and their natural instincts were to get as far up the pitch as they could.'

Harford, in fact, admits that he opposed the signing of Sutton. He agreed with Dalglish that it was in Blackburn's interests to stockpile players of that quality, if only to increase competition for first-team places, and that Blackburn's reliance on Shearer could easily rebound on them. Apart from the possibility of his sustaining another serious injury, Shearer, who had the same agent as his England colleague David Platt, was known to be thinking about one day following Platt into the Italian League. But Harford had reservations about Sutton as a possible replacement for Shearer – he felt that Sutton's best position was centre-half.

He also had doubts about whether Sutton could be transformed into another Newell. 'Chris is a good player,' Newell says, 'and it's not as if he didn't try to play the way Ray wanted. I wouldn't call him a selfish player – he did his bit. But, if you have it in your mind that you are being asked to do something which is going to detract from what you think you're good at, then you're not going to be that effective. It's the same in any walk of life.'

Even at the height of Rovers' success, it was difficult to avoid forming the impression that Shearer and Sutton were somehow working independently of each other. Following a 3–0 win at Aston Villa, where Shearer had scored two of the goals and Sutton the other, Villa's central-defender Paul McGrath commented: 'I am not sure that they combine that well together yet.' This apparent contradiction was endorsed by Shearer himself when he said: 'You mustn't let goals overshadow performances, and sometimes they can, can't they? Because we have got goals doesn't mean that we have been playing well as a partnership.'

Even more intriguing was the suggestion that the two men did not get on as people either. There were even rumours of a feud between them, rumours that became so strong that Shearer felt moved to discuss the relationship publicly. 'I have heard it said that Chris and I don't get on,' he stated in December, 'but that's nonsense, absolute rubbish.'

If there *was* any friction between them, it is unlikely to have been over money, at least initially. Although Sutton's Blackburn contract reportedly brought him £12,000 a week, £2,000 more than Shearer was said to be getting, the club quickly took the initiative to amend the latter's contract accordingly. But, despite their financial parity, one thing that seemed clear is that they portrayed considerably different images to their dressing-room colleagues.

Sutton could come across as a withdrawn figure, which led those who worked with him to think that he might be finding it difficult to come to terms with the pressures of his £5 million price tag and playing for a club at which expectations were so high. It is often said that the most successful players are liable to be the ones who are the most insecure. Shearer would seem to disprove the view but, in Sutton's case, Newell recalls: 'He did let things get to him. All I needed to keep my confidence high at Blackburn was for

Kenny to keep selecting me. For me, to have someone like Dalglish showing faith in you should be enough for any professional footballer. But Chris, well, it was surprising how low he could seem at times.'

In a remarkable interview with Shearer and himself in the *News of the World* (the newspaper to which Shearer was contracted). Shearer said: 'Right from the moment Chris arrived at Ewood Park, I told him what to expect – that it would not be all a bed of roses. There is the hate mail, the terrace chanting, the knowledge that although you never set the multi-million-pound fee, people still hold you responsible. But I have always insisted to myself that no one is worth the kind of money paid for us. The people that deserve such rewards are doctors, nurses and firemen. Us? We're simply footballers. I always rated it as a privilege to be known as England's most expensive footballer, but when the snipers start taking aim, I just duck and laugh it off. I'm lucky because I reckon I'm quite strong mentally. Remember, I had to travel 350 miles south from Newcastle to Southampton when I was just 15, and that really toughens you up. There were plenty of times when I was homesick. But to be a footballer at that age, and train with men, you have to act like a man. I got married when I was 20, and I was a dad a year later. That makes you grow up fast.'

Sutton, three years older than Shearer, said: 'Alan's been very, very helpful to me. He has watched over me a little, been a bit like a father figure to me at times. Yet I still have to admit that I've become a little paranoid, and I don't think people can blame me for that. The strain of coming to Blackburn as a £5 million player was tough enough to deal with, but I got a taste of the pressures at Norwich, when things could get unpleasant and even dangerous. I'd go into a bar, and there would always be somebody trying to wind me up to get me going. In a situation like that, you walk away and get called a chicken. That kind of insult can be tough for a young bloke to shrug off.'

That was not the only interview in which Sutton drew attention to the 'pressures' of his position, and his 'paranoia'. On the face of it, Sutton's problems did not seem to have an adverse effect on his performances – far from it. In the opening five months of the season especially, the 'SAS' proved so threatening that Newell, having returned to full fitness in September following a close-season knee operation, was able to make only two Premiership appearances as a substitute. By the season's halfway stage, Shearer and Sutton had scored 17 and 13 times respectively in 21 matches, from which Blackburn had taken 49 points. One match which summed up the pair's influence better than most was the 4–0 win at QPR on 26 November, when Sutton scored the opening goal and Shearer got a hat-trick (through a close-range finish from Graeme Le Saux's free-kick, a penalty and a spectacular 35-yard drive that appeared to take the paint off the underside of the QPR bar). That victory, on a day when Manchester United were held to a goalless draw at Arsenal, enabled Blackburn to replace United at the top of the table, a position they held for the rest of the season.

Sutton, however, was unable to maintain his scoring prowess, which meant that Blackburn had to rely on Shearer more heavily than ever. In the second half of the season, Shearer scored as many goals as he had in the first, but Sutton managed only two; and Blackburn could take only 40 points from those last 21 matches.

'Alan had to take more on his shoulders, really,' Newell says. 'Chris seemed to lose a bit of confidence. He wasn't going past people and creating chances as he did before, and he was no real help to Alan because of it. Before, it didn't matter if he wasn't going deep and getting the ball into Alan because he was creating chances for Alan in other ways, with his knock-downs or shots and headers that were rebounding to Alan, for example. So Alan was going through four or five matches without scoring, Chris wasn't scoring at all and we were struggling. The longer it went on, the worse it got, and the worse the team played.'

Nonetheless, Sutton continued to keep Newell out of the team – and, though Shearer himself clearly had cause to disagree with the decision, the end just about justified the means. Newell, who made only 12 Premiership appearances in all that season, ten as substitute, says: 'It became frustrating for me because I thought that the way Alan and I combined might make a difference to the side. But we were still scraping out results, and I think Kenny's attitude was: "If it ain't broke, don't fix it."'

No doubt Dalglish was encouraged by the fact that Manchester United, despite producing another British record transfer deal with the signing of striker Andy Cole from Newcastle for £7 million on 10 January, did not look in perfect running order either. Apart from his five goals in United's astonishing 9–0 demolition of Ipswich in March, Cole struggled to adjust to his new team's style of play. Not that this was the only headache for United: shortly after the acquisition of Cole, United's centre-forward Mark Hughes was forced out of action for three months with a knee injury; and, most alarming of all for the Old Trafford giants, was that Eric Cantona then plunged the club into their biggest controversy for years as a result of that infamous kung-fu attack on a Crystal Palace supporter in the 1–1 draw at Selhurst Park on 25 January. In view of the furore this created, not to mention Cantona's suspension for the rest of the season, United did well to keep as closely in touch with Blackburn as they did.

Over the second half of the season Rovers also had the advantage of having only the Championship in their sights. In addition to their UEFA Cup first-round defeat by Trelleborg, they had been beaten by Newcastle in the third round of the FA Cup and by Liverpool in the fourth round of the Coca-Cola Cup – a match best remembered for Ian Rush's hat-trick and an unsavoury clash between Shearer and his old Southampton friend, Neil Ruddock, which resulted in both being booked. In contrast, United had the distractions of the European Champions' League and an FA Cup run which took them to the final.

Blackburn, though, did give them some encouragement. At one stage it looked as if they would run away with the title, especially when Shearer came up with the sort of performance that he produced in the 2–1 win at home to Chelsea on 18 March. Chelsea took a third-minute lead through Mark Stein, but Shearer scored the equaliser in the 16th minute – his 100th league goal – and supplied the pass from which Tim Sherwood put Blackburn ahead. That win put Blackburn six points ahead of United, a gap that was to remain the following day as United lost 2–0 to Liverpool. By 4 April, when Blackburn won 1–0 at QPR (courtesy of Sutton) the gulf between the two was stretched to eight points, with six matches left.

It was then that Blackburn, having yet to prove to themselves that they could hold a Championship lead, showed signs of choking on it. In their next four matches, they allowed Leeds to come from behind at Elland Road to hold them to a 1–1 draw, lost 3–2 at home to Manchester City and, following a 2–1 home win over Crystal Palace, were beaten 2–0 at West Ham. United, who beat Leicester and drew with Chelsea during this period, went on to win their two matches in hand – against Coventry and Sheffield Wednesday – to narrow Blackburn's lead to two points.

In addition to thinking that United were likely to overtake Blackburn, a number of professional observers and neutral fans gave the impression of hoping this would happen. Although United had lost a number of points in the popularity stakes as a result of their refusal to boot Cantona out of Old Trafford following his behaviour at Crystal Palace, they were much the more individualistic and attractive of the two teams. Perhaps typical of the way Blackburn were perceived was Gary Lineker's view of Dalglish's troops in his column for *The Observer* on 7 May.

He wrote: 'Dalglish needs to discourage his team from over-indulgence with the long ball. Where earlier in the season the direct route was always a useful option, over the past few weeks it has become something of an obsession. Blackburn's play has become somewhat stereotyped and easy to defend against. With Jason Wilcox [Blackburn's injured left-side attacking player] sorely missed, and Stuart Ripley [their right-side attacking player] totally out of sorts, opponents have little to fear from Blackburn's flanks. Without Blackburn lacking the ability in wide positions that Manchester United possess, opposing back fours can concentrate on nullifying Blackburn's real threat. By shutting down the spaces between centre-half and full-back that Shearer and Sutton exploit so brilliantly, Blackburn's potency is severely reduced. The men from Ewood Park need to be more patient with their build-up. Retaining possession will allow their full-backs added time and more opportunities to get forward and contribute to Blackburn's attacking play, and help prevent an over-reliance on the "SAS" partnership.'

As valid as Lineker's comments were, the fact that Blackburn were 'over-reliant' on Shearer was something that the player relished. In the light of the pressure that United had put on them with those wins over Coventry and Sheffield Wednesday, Blackburn clearly needed Shearer to come up with something special again in their next match, at Newcastle on 8 May; and he did not disappoint. Only one goal was scored, and it was scored by him; the importance of it was fully seen two days later, when United beat Southampton to cut Blackburn's advantage back to two points with one match left.

All of this set up a finale as exciting as any there has been in English football, with Blackburn knowing that even a draw at Liverpool would not be enough to earn them the title they craved if United, who had a superior goal difference, achieved the seemingly less difficult result of a win at lowly West Ham.

Despite another Shearer goal, Blackburn lost 2–1 – but at Upton Park, United, despite putting enough pressure on the Hammers and creating enough chances to win, were held to a 1–1 draw.

All this raised the question of what the outcome of that title race would have been had United had Shearer – and, in view of his aversion to putting himself into a position in which he might stagnate, how long Blackburn could keep him. His contract was due to expire in the summer of 1996, and amidst their Championship celebrations, there were clear indications that he was unwilling to commit himself to the club beyond that. He was quoted as saying: 'I signed a four-year contract and unless Blackburn decide they want to sell me, I will be a Rovers player next season. I am ready to sit down and talk right now. All I have said about my future is that I wanted to concentrate on winning the Championship with Blackburn. The next thing was having a successful European tournament with England next summer. One half is out of the way. Let me get on with the other half and I will have an answer for you.'

With typical shrewdness, Shearer did sign an extended contract, to take him up to the summer of 1999, but this time he insisted on a get-out clause. In common with all his other major career decisions, it was to prove spot on.

CHAPTER NINE

Wembley Heroics

Alan Shearer's ability to find sunshine behind the darkest of clouds was again put to the test in the 1995–96 season. It was a season in which the house that Jack built – the multi-million-pound Jack Walker empire that now housed the Championship trophy – revealed disturbing cracks in its structure. In defence of the trophy, Blackburn made the worst start since Everton had 25 years earlier, suffering four defeats and a home draw in their opening six matches, and eventually finishing seventh – their lowest position since their return to the top flight. Blackburn were knocked out of the Coca-Cola Cup by Leeds in the fourth round, and the FA Cup by Ipswich in the third round.

Even more disappointing for them was their bottom-of-the-table position in the European Champions' League, following just one win in six matches against Spartak Moscow, Rosenborg and Legia Warsaw. As if this meagre return in a group that was considered the weakest of the four Champions' League sections was not embarrassing enough, Blackburn invited added criticism with the lack of discipline that marked their 3–0 defeat by Spartak Moscow in Russia. For a team like Blackburn, who had always been categorised as machine-like, the sight of Graeme Le Saux and David Batty trading blows with each other in that match (which led to both players being heavily fined by the club) was mind-boggling.

Shearer, though, was a man apart. He again topped the 30-goal mark, ending the season with a total of 36 (31 in the Premiership) to become the first player to find the net 30 times or more in three successive seasons. The belief that he had carried Blackburn was difficult to dispute when his 1995–96 record was set against that of Graham Fenton, their next highest scorer. Fenton, bought from West Bromwich Albion for £1.5 million in November 1995, ended up with a total of just six.

Having gone so long without scoring for England that it became an obsession (at least with the critics), Shearer at last came good in that department in Euro 96. He received one of the most remarkable offers ever made to a 26-year-old player, that of becoming Blackburn's player-manager; and, of course, there was his eventual £15 million transfer to Newcastle.

The opportunity to become the figurehead of the Blackburn team off the field as well as on it came on the initiative of Ray Harford, who had taken over as team manager before the start of the season when Kenny Dalglish moved into the role of Director of Football. Harford proposed to Jack Walker that the striker take on Dalglish's old job, and that Harford revert to his former position as assistant manager.

Most managers might have found it astonishing that Harford was prepared to demote himself. Walker himself asked Harford: 'Are you sure you know what you're doing?' But Harford, a man rather more sensitive about the fortunes of Blackburn than he was about his ego, was convinced that his plan was in the club's best interests. The only way he could see Blackburn continuing to move forward was for Shearer, having indicated that he felt he had reached the end of the road with the club, to be handed a challenge big enough for him to change his mind. To Harford, the logic behind the idea was not just related to Shearer's goalscoring ability. It also had something to do with the belief that the player, through his special rapport with Walker, might have a bigger influence on the tycoon than he could when it came to signing the players Harford felt were necessary to maintain Blackburn's progress.

It was no secret that, even for Walker, there was a limit to how much he was prepared to underwrite the club's expenditure. Right from the start of the Dalglish-Harford partnership, Walker made it clear to the pair that, while he was happy to provide the cash to give the club its initial impetus, he expected Rovers to become more self-sufficient within five years. This made perfect sense in principle. But Blackburn, a middle-of-the-range Premiership club in crowd potential, were never going to generate as much money under their own steam as their big-city rivals such as Manchester United, Arsenal and Liverpool, so once their ability to compete on level terms with such clubs in transfer fees and wages was diminished, how could they expect to keep ahead of them? More to the point was the question of how long they could rely on Shearer, without giving him the right back-up.

In a sense Blackburn and Walker had made a rod for their own backs with the signings of such players. The Blackburn team had arguably played above itself to win the title, yet this made little difference to the expectations of their fans. Harford likened the speed with which the team had been put together to that of 'building a house with no proper walls'. Unfortunately for him, he became manager at a time when the money that could have provided stronger walls was no longer in such plentiful supply.

Hit by injuries and badly needing to improve the depth of his squad, Harford did spend more than £11.5 million in the transfer market that season, yet the outlay covered six players, of whom only one (Gary Flitcroft of Manchester City) cost more than £3 million, and one (Chris Coleman of Crystal Palace) cost more than £2 million. He was denied the chance to make any what he called 'really big' buys, the sort of extra-special players who could take the club onto a fresh plateau and, equally importantly, convince Shearer that Blackburn were moving in the right direction. There was an opportunity for the club to do this before the start of the season when David Platt, then England's captain and Shearer's room-mate on international trips, signalled his intention to return to English football from Sampdoria. Platt was valued at between £4.5 million and £5 million and, although Harford was keen on bringing him to Ewood, Walker was concerned that the player was too old to have a similarly high resale value. Platt eventually ended up at Arsenal and the only other area in which he and Shearer were able to join forces, outside their England appearances, concerned Shearer's decision to follow Platt into the Jaguar owners' club with the purchase of a £47,000, 155mph XJR model.

Whether Shearer felt as comfortable in the front seat of the spluttering Blackburn machine was open to doubt. Such was Harford's desire to stimulate him that, while Chris Sutton started the season as Shearer's striking partner, Harford had no hesitation in bringing Mike Newell back at Sutton's expense when things were not working out, 'to keep Alan happy'. At the end of the season, Harford, again with Shearer in mind, tried to buy the French international centre-forward, Christophe Dugarry from Bordeaux. But while Blackburn were prepared to pay his transfer fee, they balked at the player's personal demands.

It seems churlish to blame Walker for any of this. As Ray Harford points out, he did more for the club than almost any boardroom figure in the game's history. At the same time, insiders suggest that the longer Walker was in command, the more he started to have his own opinions on potential signings, and that he became no less of a hard-headed businessmen in his approach to Blackburn as any of the other mega-wealthy figures at the helm of Premiership clubs.

'I'm not sure it would be entirely fair to say that Jack did not want to spend any more money after we won the Championship,' Harford says. 'But basically he took the view that we had enough top-class players and did not need any more.'

It is understood that the change in Walker's attitude started even when Dalglish was manager and that it caused the Scot to become increasingly disenchanted with the job – not to mention wary about subjecting himself to the sort of pressures that had affected him when he was manager of Liverpool. In that respect, Harford played a considerable part in ensuring the necessary managerial stability at Ewood Park. Some 12 months before Blackburn won the title, Dalglish told the board that instead of signing a new contract, he would prefer to switch to a week-to-week agreement. Blackburn were inevitably unhappy about the element of uncertainty in such an arrangement and suggested to Harford that he should take over. Harford refused, out of loyalty to Dalglish, and then persuaded his partner that the pair should carry on as before. It was inevitable that there would come a time when Harford, who did most of the work with the players, would start to get frustrated about not having the final say on matters such as team selection, especially as he was receiving offers to be manager of other clubs. So the switch that saw Harford become Blackburn's manager, and Dalglish take on a broader but less pressurised role, seemed to suit the two men perfectly.

Harford, though, admits that he allowed the job to change him as a person; to cause him to retreat into himself. He says: 'It's totally different to being an assistant manager. When I worked with Kenny, I was the organiser, the one who did the screaming and shouting at the players. But, as I didn't pick the team, and was not involved in their contract negotiations and things like that they could confide in me. When I became manager, I felt I had to distance myself from them and I probably took it to the extreme. One thing I definitely should not have done was to stop taking the training. I just isolated myself, and without that sort of day-to-day contact with the players, my personality changed.'

One of the most damaging aspects of that was a blow-up with David Batty, which led to the player being banished to the reserves and, eventually, sold to Newcastle. Harford is unwilling to reveal the reasons for the falling-out, but says: 'I did not handle that situation very well. The thing was that I really felt under severe pressure, especially at the time of the European Champions' League matches. My self-esteem was so low I was blaming myself for everything.'

On top of all that, Harford felt he also suffered from having been promoted from within, a situation that had been repeated from the three previous clubs at which he had became manager – Fulham,

159

Luton and Wimbledon – and which he believed detracted from the way he was perceived at boardroom level.

Hence his brainwave about putting Shearer in charge. As with Harford, Walker looked on the player as a favourite son. If a man like Walker could be said to be star-struck about anyone, then it was his Roy of the Rovers in Blackburn's No. 9 shirt. But Shearer turned down the proposal on the grounds that he was at too early a stage in his career to contemplate taking another football route; and from that point on Blackburn's uphill battle to keep him grew ever steeper.

When Shearer left, nobody accused him of having exploited Blackburn, and nor did they have any cause to do so. He would have benefited enormously by not signing a new Blackburn contract the previous season. Though the agreement was not signed without Blackburn promising they would release him if he became unhappy at the club, and without a clause that his agent Tony Stephens could negotiate on his behalf with any club prepared to pay £10 million for him it would have made more sense for him – financially – to allow his original deal to run out. As a result of the changes in the transfer system following the Jean-Marc Bosman ruling, he could then have moved to a big foreign club on a free transfer and taken the £10 million as a signing-on fee.

So, when Shearer left Blackburn, the reaction among their fans was one of gratitude for what he had done for the club, rather than resentment or bitterness. It wasn't necessary to have a long memory to appreciate his commitment to the Blackburn cause – the previous nine months said it all.

For someone who could generally be relied upon to steer clear of controversy, the start of the season was strangely contentious for Alan Shearer. In the FA Charity Shield against Everton on 12 August, which Blackburn lost 1–0, he was accused by Everton manager Joe Royle of having attempted to 'manipulate' the referee into awarding Blackburn a penalty. Royle revealed that as the two teams walked down the players' tunnel at the end, he told Shearer:

'If you try to manipulate situations, they will go against you.' The theme was continued in Blackburn's first Premiership match – at QPR – the following Saturday, with Shearer getting the goal from a penalty awarded for what seemed no more than an accidental collision between him and David Bardsley. Later, with opposing crowds latching on to Shearer's disappointing scoring record for England as a way of getting back at him over the goals he managed against their own teams ('You'll never score for England,' they chanted), he was accused of having incited spectators at Middlesbrough. Boro supporters claimed to police that, after Shearer had scored the only goal in the Premiership match between the two clubs at Ewood Park on 16 December, he made a point of raising his arms in celebration immediately in front of the visiting supporters' section. He was totally cleared of the charge; and then highlighted the futility of crowds trying to intimidate someone as focused and astute as him when he said: 'It's water off a duck's back to me. If anything, the more the crowds bait me, the more it gees me up. It certainly doesn't bother me.'

This hardly needed to be said when you looked at his scoring record. During Blackburn's stumbling start to the season when they took just four points from their opening six Premiership matches, he scored all but one of their five goals. Immediately afterwards, he scored a hat-trick in a 5–1 home win over Coventry to bring his career total to 102 in 133 matches and thus establish the record for the quickest-ever ton in English football. This was one of five Shearer hat-tricks that season. The others came against Nottingham Forest on 18 November (7–0); West Ham on 2 December (4–2); Bolton on 3 February (3–0); and Tottenham on 16 March (3–2).

It was against Tottenham at home, on 30 December, that Shearer reached another milestone – that of becoming the first player to reach the 100-goal mark in the Premiership itself. Blackburn won 2–1 and Shearer, on his 124th Premiership appearance, grabbed the winner. In addition, there could be no prizes for guessing that the strike which brought him his record was no ordinary finish. In his report of the match in the *Sunday Times*, David Maddocks put it this way: 'Shearer's historic goal was a thing of beauty, something that he has almost made his trademark. He has the ability of a conjurer, creating things out of thin air. There seemed no danger as he received the ball from Bohinen 25 yards out. A little glance, and it was on its way in a delightful arc over Walker, the stranded Tottenham keeper.'

Tottenham's Gary Mabbutt, who'd had the unenviable job of marking him, drew further attention to Shearer's reputation for knowing all the 'tricks of the trade', when he said: 'He is a tough player, physically, to come up against. He is very strong, and he backs into you, making it look sometimes as if the defender has clattered into him. It's all part of his game. Against a lot of strikers, you try to get around them and win the ball in front of them, but it's so difficult to do that with Alan. He uses his body so well that, in the process of trying to win the ball that way, you tend to give away free-kicks.'

It was Shearer's match-winner that made the biggest impression on Mabbutt, though, especially as the striker had his back to the goal when he gained possession and Mabbutt had seemingly closed down all his shooting options. In addition to the sharpness with which Shearer turned the Spurs man, Mabbutt pointed out: 'He hit the ball when it appeared to be rolling away from him. It was an incredible strike.'

'Incredible' . . . you would make a fortune if you could receive £100 every time that is said about Shearer.

When he scored his hat-trick against Bolton, it made him the only player to have scored against all 26 teams to have played in the Premiership. Colin Todd, Bolton's manager, could only endorse what everybody else was saying about him: 'People go on about Les Ferdinand and others, but Shearer is the best. He moves so well, everything seems to revolve around him.'

But, with increasing speculation about interest from top foreign clubs in him, how long Blackburn could hold on to him was open to some doubt. Those who mixed with him in the England squad

– and had an insight into his determination to keep developing himself – might have been the least willing to place any bets on his remaining at Ewood Park for the remainder of his contract.

If ever there was any justification for him to leave Rovers, it was the belief that Blackburn's style of play had caused him to become too stereotyped, and that being in a different set-up would help him make a more effective adjustment to what was required of him in the England team. As had been shown by their handful of appearances in Europe, Blackburn's approach to the game, while effective in English football, was less likely to stand them in good stead against more studious and technically accomplished teams from other countries. Shearer must also have been concerned that Blackburn did not seem likely to qualify for European competition again for a while – a situation that was bound to have an adverse effect on his learning cycle in international football.

At any level, the fact that Shearer had the constitution of an ox, and an almost freakish degree of single-mindedness, could not be dismissed. Certainly, his overall England performances were never less than satisfactory. But throughout the build-up to Euro 96, his lack of goals at this level continued to give cause for concern. In his column for *The Observer*, Lineker – an expert if ever there was one on the subject of what it takes to be a top England goalscorer – first touched on Shearer's 'problems' in March 1995. 'Shearer is only deficient in one area of his game, and that's his lack of experience against the style of football played on the Continent. I agree with Jürgen Klinsmann when he says that three goals scored in England are probably worth the same as two scored in Italy. My move to Barcelona, which brought the opportunity to face these problems [of Continental teams defending with more depth and sometimes using man-to-man markers] every week, was invaluable.'

In October that year, after Colombia had become the sixth successive side to stop Shearer scoring, Lineker again spotlighted his need to learn about the game at this level. Referring to the criticism of Venables' system, Lineker pointed out that he had been in a similar situation to Shearer in the 1990 World Cup finals.

'Some of you may argue that in 1990 we nearly reached the World Cup final playing with two strikers. The truth is, Peter Beardsley has never been a genuine front man; he was more a link between the midfield and me up front.'

He added: 'Every striker, however prolific, has unproductive spells. A bigger worry, I feel, has been Shearer's inability thus far to adapt to the role of lone striker. There is no questioning the Blackburn goal machine's commitment or, indeed, his talent, but the forward's function in this England system requires more thought than effort. In the white shirt of England, Shearer continues to make the runs into wide areas that he does for his club. He does this with total honesty, believing he is helping his team. Without the support of a fellow striker, what he is in fact doing is distancing himself from his team-mates. The build-up should be through the team, with Shearer staying central and attached to his team, enabling him to be used like a wall to bounce the ball off. His runs directly towards goal should only be made when the team are well into the opposing half.

'With Blackburn continuing to ask their top man to chase the long ball, the only place Shearer will receive an education is with the national side. He will have to learn fast because Venables has neither the desire to change his system, nor the time to wait before he is forced to try someone else.'

Publicly, Terry Venables did not seem too bothered about Shearer's international scoring record; neither did the player himself. Venables, faced with a growing campaign for Shearer to be axed from the side, repeatedly drew attention to the striker's value to England in other aspects of the game. Nonetheless, it is not unreasonable to suggest that Shearer, with his fierce pride and determination to conquer all his flaws, will have found this blot on his England CV more unacceptable than anyone.

To his credit, Shearer, in his public utterances on the subject, refused to attribute his problems to the restrictions imposed on him as a goalscorer by his 'Lone Ranger' role. While he appeared to agree with Gary Lineker (that it was up to him to adjust to

England, not the other way around), Ray Harford said: 'He needs the right support, but the thing I found with him when we [Blackburn] tried to play with one up front early on was that he did not like to detach himself from the play. If we were developing an attack down one side, then we really wanted Alan to come away, and sometimes do nothing because just by standing there he could keep defenders occupied. But supporters can get the impression that you're lazy when you do that, and this goes against Alan's nature – I think that Alan feels he has to be seen to be busy. Also, the more isolated you are up front, the more you need to be able to vary your pace, to be able to be standing still one moment, and then suddenly go to quick and then lightning quick. Alan doesn't have that blistering pace, and one way he can counteract this is to keep on the move, keep his momentum up.'

In fact, for all the theories put forward to explain Shearer's goal drought with the national side, the eventual solution to the problem turned out to be a simple one. As Harford said, he needed the right support, and this was provided – eventually – by the inclusion of Teddy Sheringham as his regular striking partner.

It seems likely that Shearer, who entered the Euro 96 fray on a run of 12 England matches without scoring, would have had a rather different story to tell if Sheringham had been alongside him more often. The first time they played together was against the United States in September 1994, when Shearer scored both goals in a 2–0 England win, but the significance of the performance was inevitably clouded by the poor standard of the opposition. Terry Venables summed it up when he said that Shearer, then with five goals in 11 England matches, could easily have doubled the figure in that one game. At any event, Venables saw no reason to make hard and fast judgements about the players available to him at that stage, and continued experimenting.

Prior to Euro 96, there were only six other occasions in England's 20 build-up matches under Venables that Shearer and Sheringham were seen together in the same team – and on only three of those occasions did they start a match together, namely the

Umbro Cup matches against Sweden (3–3) and Brazil (1–3) in June 1994, and the game against Switzerland (3–1) in November 1995.

As the 1995–96 season progressed, the more Shearer's supporters must have felt that his place in the side might be in jeopardy. Sheringham was known to be greatly admired by Venables, who had signed him for Tottenham from Nottingham Forest when he was Spurs manager; Ferdinand, bought by Newcastle from QPR for £6 million before the start of the season, was going great guns with his new club. But Venables gave off different vibes. In one interview, in which he was commenting on English strikers generally, he said that he had looked upon Shearer as the best of the bunch long before he became England coach, and had subsequently seen no reason to change his opinion.

The first clue from Venables that Shearer and Sheringham would end up as his preferred front-line pairing came after the draw against Portugal in December, when Shearer and Ferdinand had operated together for the first time. Ferdinand, who had to be taken off because of a hamstring injury and was replaced by Beardsley, was far from disappointed with his performance. 'I thought I did well and I enjoyed it,' he said. 'I believe I proved that Alan Shearer and I can play together.' Venables was more guarded: 'Les and Alan were successful up to a point. It was their first game together and they worked hard. They caused danger in the air and on the ground, but I do say you need a bit of depth.'

That word 'depth' was the key one, as Ray Harford had acknowledged with his misgivings about having two centre-forwards like Sutton and Shearer together at Blackburn, and his preference of Mike Newell as Shearer's partner because of the former's ability to drop off into deeper positions. When it came to strikers who could complement Shearer in this way, Sheringham, a centre-forward lacking the pace to get beyond opposing defences, was the de luxe version. 'He is not as mobile as a lot of other strikers,' Harford admits, 'but he is exceptionally clever – and Alan reacts to clever people.'

In England's opening Euro 96 matches, Venables' players,

battling to come to terms with the physical and emotional strain of competing in such a tournament after a gruelling domestic season, needed all the cleverness they could muster. England's apparent advantage in being the hosts of the competition, and playing all their matches at Wembley, was somewhat misleading when set against the pressure imposed on them by the expectations of the media and the public. This, after all, was the biggest sporting event staged in England since the 1966 World Cup and the excitement it created – even among those with no real interest in football in normal circumstances – could best be described as intoxicating.

It was only to be expected, therefore, that as Sir Alf Ramsey's triumphant squad had found in 1966, it took Venables' troops time to get into their stride in a preliminary group which included Switzerland, Scotland and Holland. But as the competition progressed, the stronger England seemed to become – and the more we were inclined to believe that, with David Seaman and Tony Adams at the back, Gazza in midfield and Shearer up front, anything was possible.

If Shearer himself was in need of a lift, then he could hardly have picked a better time to get it. England were clearly struggling to impose themselves in their opening match against Switzerland on 8 June when, midway through the first half, he received a pass from Paul Ince in a position just in front of the opponents' last line of defence. The ball surprised the Swiss, who had expected Ince to play it out wide to Darren Anderton; but it came as no surprise to Ince, nor to any of the other England players, when Shearer made light of a tight shooting angle with a tremendous drive that beat the keeper by his near post.

Relief for England – and particularly for Shearer, whose immediate reaction at breaking his scoring hoodoo with the national side was to glance to the heavens as if offering thanks that his prayers had been answered. The Swiss, too, experienced that feeling as England later wilted and Turkyilmaz grabbed a late equaliser from a fortuitous penalty awarded for handball against Stuart Pearce.

It was England's turn to be lucky in their next clash, with Scotland, on 15 June. After a first half in which the Scots were the more impressive of the two sides, Shearer again scored the first goal, bustling past his Blackburn colleague Colin Hendry to head in Gary Neville's excellent cross in the 53rd minute.

But then Arsenal's goalkeeper, David Seaman, took over the role of England hero with a brilliant save from Gordon Durie and a penalty save from Scotland's captain, Gary McAllister. And, finally, it was Paul Gascoigne's turn. Shearer had scored some breathtaking goals in his time, but even he might have been envious of the one that his fellow Geordie struck in this match. In his report of the game in *The Observer*, Paul Wilson wrote: 'If the Tartan Army at the same end of the ground [where McAllister failed to convert his spot-kick] thought they could not be more dejected, they were mistaken. In under two minutes, Goram was plucking the ball out of his net and England were 2–0 in front. The Scottish Footballer of the Year [Gascoigne] was to blame, skipping gleefully onto an Anderton pass, showing a delightful first touch to lift the ball over Hendry's head, then nipping around the big defender to volley decisively past Goram. Say what you like about Gazza, but the boy can certainly play.'

If you thought at that moment that the Wembley rendition of England's Euro 96 song 'Football's Coming Home' had reached its most vibrant level, it was nothing compared with the gusto with which it was belted out by the packed crowd three days later when England faced Holland.

This time, the attention was focused very much on Shearer and Sheringham. The two teams, level on points at the top of the group, three ahead of Switzerland and Scotland, only needed a draw to clinch their places in the quarter-finals. Because of the complicated criteria for separating teams who finished on the same number of points, Scotland could only qualify at the expense of Holland, a scenario that required England to beat Holland and the Scots to get the better of Switzerland by two goals. Likewise, in the event of a Dutch win, England could only be prevented from qualifying by the Swiss.

England, though, were in no mood to take the easy way out by playing for a draw. Against a Dutch team undermined by disharmony in the camp – an old problem for them – Shearer and co seized the initiative midway through the first half, and went on to produce the most dazzling performance seen by an England team in years.

Shearer could have scored after just seven minutes, producing a shot through a thicket of legs that was cleared off the line. He was luckier 14 minutes later, when Paul Ince was brought down in the area by Holland's captain Danny Blind, and Shearer drove the kick low past the keeper to set his team alight. By half-time, Holland could easily have been in the lead themselves, following three chances created by Dennis Bergkamp. But the Dutch were then destroyed by three more England goals in the space of just 13 minutes. The first, after 50 minutes, came via a Sheringham header from Gascoigne's corner. Gazza was also involved in the next goal, supplying a pass which put Sheringham in a reasonable scoring position, but which the Tottenham striker unselfishly diverted to the even better-placed Shearer on his right. The Dutch defence was in tatters and Shearer, taking advantage of the keeper's struggle to adjust his position following Sheringham's lay-off, beat him with a resounding shot inside his near post. It was now carnival time, and the Dutch defence was again in disarray as Sheringham pounced on a deflection from a Darren Anderton shot to get England's fourth.

The quarter-final against Spain on 22 June provided a glimpse of the other side of the coin for England's SAS team, with the well-organised Spanish defence limiting them to only a handful of chances and only one (for Sheringham) that could be described as clear-cut. This, indeed, was an entirely different match from the one England had experienced against the Dutch; it was a game in which England had to draw on all their reserves of character to avoid going under. Quite apart from containing the England attack, Spain had the best scoring opportunities. The Spaniards had two 'goals' disallowed for offside, and England also had a let-off in

possibility of his remaining at Blackburn, the main attractions for him were Manchester United, Liverpool and Newcastle. All three, together with Arsenal, had expressed a strong desire to buy him, with Manchester United having been the first of the group to broach the subject with Blackburn – in May – and were widely regarded as the favourites. However, while Shearer's conversation with the manager on the subject did not produce anything conclusive in the player's deliberations, Harford had the feeling that Liverpool could be in the strongest position to land him.

All three clubs had a great deal going for them as far as Shearer was concerned, so to a certain extent Harford played the role of Devil's Advocate. For example, one of Shearer's guidelines was that it had to be a club he could help lift to success and, in that department, the challenge for him at Manchester United – who were already winning virtually everything in sight – seemed to Harford to be less stimulating than those at Liverpool and Newcastle. Moreover, the feeling that he had much more to lose than to gain at United was heightened by the abuse he had taken from the Old Trafford crowd following his decision to sign for Blackburn instead of United when he left Southampton. Shearer is an intensely proud man with a strong sense of personal integrity, as Harford acknowledged when he mentioned the possibility of a move to United being construed as 'two-faced'.

Still, in addition to United's stature, Shearer had been impressed by manager Alex Ferguson when he met him a few days earlier. Another plus point about United, and one that applied even more to Liverpool, was that Shearer could continue living in Southport – an area in which he had found it easy to lead a normal family life and which, indeed, had become something of a sanctuary for him.

Adding to Shearer's dilemma was the emotional attraction of Newcastle, the dream of returning to his roots and working with the man – Kevin Keegan – he had idolised as a boy; and the fact that Jack Walker was willing to move heaven and earth to keep him at Blackburn.

Harford stepped into the background after his meeting with

Shearer, with Blackburn's chairman Robert Coar and Walker taking charge of the affair, and claims that he had no knowledge of the chain of events that led Shearer to Newcastle. One source claims that Walker offered Shearer £10,000 a week extra to remain with Blackburn for one more season and that the player, having agreed to consider the proposal, was 'disappointed' with Walker's 'attitude' to him when they met to discuss it further. 'Kevin Keegan was in contact with Alan then,' the source adds, 'and he caught him at the right time. Kevin is an exceptionally persuasive person – you can't help but be influenced by his enthusiasm and warmth – and during a period when Alan was at his most indecisive, this was what won the day for Newcastle.'

Whatever the truth of the matter, the one thing that is clear is that men with Walker's power and wealth do not take kindly to being seen to be beaten. Though Walker was referred to affectionately as 'Uncle Jack' among the Ewood Park staff, the image became less appropriate when he had to resign himself to losing Shearer. As Shearer was under contract to Blackburn, they had the upper hand in the transfer negotiations – and Walker, donning the tough business hat that had stood him in such good stead in the steel industry, was no slouch in capitalising on it.

As it turned out, Shearer could not have gone to Old Trafford even if he had desperately wanted to – because Walker opposed such a move on the grounds of Blackburn's local rivalry with United. The price Newcastle were pushed to pay for him – well in excess of the £10 million at which the bidding had begun – also spiked the guns of Liverpool, another club too close to Ewood Park for Walker's comfort.

It was only to be expected that the following season would be an even more difficult one for Blackburn, especially when the departure of Shearer was followed by the resignation of a beleaguered Harford in November. It was only to be expected, too, that Shearer would keep going onwards and upwards.

CHAPTER TEN

Case for the Defence

At Upton Park on Tuesday, 6 May 1997, West Ham's Slaven Bilic, poised to become Britain's most expensive defender, managed to claim another rare distinction – that of becoming one of the few players to stop Britain's most expensive striker scoring.

Short of a disaster against Shearer, Bilic's £6 million transfer to Everton in the summer was inevitable. The Croatian, one of the most impressive of the foreign stars in the Premiership, had already made it clear that he wanted to join a bigger and more successful club at the end of the season. Of all the clubs who wanted him, Everton, who had made a £4.5 million bid for him in March and had virtually first option on him, were clearly in no mood to lose out for the sake of a million or two.

Nonetheless, if Bilic was looking for something extra special to put on his CV, then West Ham's goalless draw with Newcastle – only the seventh time Newcastle had failed to find the opposing net in a total of 50 matches – was manna from heaven for him.

As far as scoring opportunities were concerned, it was a much better 90 minutes for West Ham's centre-forward, John Hartson, than it was for Shearer, who spent most of his time battling for balls that were no more than scraps. Such was Shearer's frustration that just before half-time, while chasing back to stop John Moncur doing any damage to the Newcastle defence, he caught the West Ham player with a rash tackle that caused the midfielder to be carried off with damaged ankle ligaments, and himself to be booked.

Bilic, however, felt he could not afford to take his eyes off Shearer for a second. On one occasion, the defender, having dispossessed Faustino Asprilla deep in West Ham's half and then created the angle for a forward pass by hooking the ball over the Colombian striker, suddenly caught sight of Shearer in a perfect position to capitalise on a slip-up. During a break in play shortly afterwards, he remarked to Shearer: 'I now know what your best quality is. You are always there, like a snake waiting to pounce, aren't you?'

'Yeah,' his opponent replied, smiling.

Bilic was given a better example of Shearer's predatory instincts 19 minutes from the end, when the Newcastle striker beat him to a corner to get in an outstanding header that, to everyone's amazement, the West Ham keeper Ludo Miklosko somehow turned over the bar. 'He pulled me down by my shirt,' Bilic says. 'Oh, he's very clever – a very, very clever player.'

That comment – and Shearer's 28 goals in 39 league and cup matches for Newcastle – only partly explains why those who threw up their hands in horror over his transfer were eventually moved to agree that he might have been a bargain. When it came to 'cleverness', Shearer was in good company with his Newcastle manager, Kevin Keegan, and most notably Newcastle's chairman, Sir John Hall. Even at a cost of a £15 million transfer fee, and a five-year contract reportedly worth £9 million to the player, the deal that brought him to St James's Park did make sense for a club of this stature, not least because of their plans to build a new 75,000-seater stadium to replace the 36,000-capacity St James's Park. Football being as important as it is in the North-east, Hall felt that with the right big-name players, it was possible for Newcastle matches in the new arena to attract sell-out crowds almost every time, and produce gate receipts of around £100 million each season.

Football-wise, Hall, the most dominant and dynamic of the new breed of high-powered figures in control of England's leading clubs, knew that his outlay on Shearer would be wiped out in a stroke if Newcastle were to go on and win the Championship and do well in the European Champions' League, two targets that were worth more than £20 million. He also knew that Shearer was capable of generating a massive income for Newcastle in other ways.

Thanks to their TV deal with BSkyB and the BBC, clubs like Newcastle – experiencing a greater public exposure than ever before – had started to strike it rich not just through their direct income from this source, but also in replica kit sales and other merchandising avenues. A spokesman for Newcastle's marketing department was quoted as saying: 'Within a week of the Shearer signing, we sold 6,000 shirts bearing his name. We expect demand to increase. From a purely commercial point of view, just having Shearer at the club is worth £1 million a year.'

Significantly, the buying of Shearer came little more than a month after Premiership clubs agreed to accept an astonishing new BSkyB-BBC deal worth £743 million over four years – more than double the previous figure for a five-year agreement. In *Sunday Business*, Dominic Turnbull, pointing out that the clubs who have most matches televised live get the most money, and that the particularly attractive teams will benefit further when the pay-per-view system is introduced, pinpointed another major factor in Hall's thinking: Newcastle's prospective flotation on the Stock Exchange. 'The City sees the Shearer deal as a sound investment. Newcastle are certain to go public soon, and the £15 million on the player will translate to £30 million on the capitalisation.' This, of course, was a language that few football professionals – and fans – would fully understand. Far easier for them to grasp was what Shearer was capable of producing on the field.

Strangely, despite his record and Newcastle's reputation as one of Britain's most adventurous and skilful attacking teams, some felt that he would not stand out there as much as he had at Blackburn; that, with so many superb individualists around him at Newcastle, he was likely to be less of a focal point than he was at Rovers. This argument was supported by the scoring records of the two teams the previous season, when Shearer scored 31 of Blackburn's 56 Premiership goals, while Newcastle's haul of 62 was shared between 12 players. Malcolm Macdonald, the former Newcastle and England centre-forward – in many ways, Newcastle's Shearer of the 1970s – wondered where the service to Shearer was going to come from. 'I was fortunate in having a wonderful passer of the ball in Terry Hibbitt in midfield,' he recalls. 'All I used to say to him: "When you see my backside, Terry, just knock the ball in front of me." There is no one like him in the present Newcastle side – if there was, I would think that Shearer or Ferdinand could get 40 to 50 goals a season, never mind 30. Shearer will get his share of goals, but he will have to rely on these coming mainly as a result of the general attacking pressure of the team.'

In a season in which he had two one-month spells out of the team because of injury, Shearer was again about to prove his ability to adapt. Up to the sensational end of Kevin Keegan's reign as manager in January, when Keegan decided he'd had enough of the pressures of the job, Shearer's place in this most uninhibited of teams brought him 17 goals in 24 matches. The appointment of Kenny Dalglish as Keegan's successor led to radical changes in Newcastle's first-team personnel and style of play, yet Shearer's scoring average – nine goals in 14 matches – showed little change.

But then Dalglish, knowing the player so well from their Blackburn days together, cannot have expected anything else. Almost immediately he took over, Dalglish must have had a sense of déjà vu. In his first match as Newcastle manager, at Aston Villa on 11 January, Shearer scored his team's first goal, holding off the challenge of Steve Staunton, from Peter Beardsley's pass, and beating the Villa keeper Mark Bosnich with a shot of trademark power and precision. Once Lee Clark had made it 2–0 shortly afterwards, however, Newcastle, reverting to their self-destructive habits of old, allowed Villa to fight back for a 2–2 draw.

Dalglish's first Newcastle match at home came five days later, when Charlton were the visitors for an FA Cup third-round replay. Newcastle struggled to get the better of the First Division side, who had the temerity not only to look Newcastle's equals for much of the contest but also to cancel out the first-half lead Lee Clark gave the Magpies to push the tie into extra time. It seemed on the cards that the game would go to a penalty shoot-out – but in the 100th minute, Dalglish's so-called 'prodigal son' came up with yet another of his special goals, an explosive shot direct from a 25-yard free-kick, to stop the manager's Tyneside welcome party turning into a wake.

Later, even Dalglish, whose usual stance towards the media is nothing if not taciturn, was positively garrulous (by his standards anyway) about Shearer: 'I am not educated enough to wax lyrical about him. After every game, you have to say something, and you can't even be original.'

West Ham apart, the only teams who had previously achieved the distinction of stopping Shearer in the league that season were Everton on 17 August, Southampton on 18 January and Middlesbrough on 22 February. West Ham's need to emulate them was particularly pronounced because the Hammers, sixth from bottom with two matches left, were still in danger of relegation. The game was no less important to Shearer and Newcastle either. Newcastle, fourth from the top with three matches left, were in a good position to clinch the runners-up spot, to earn themselves a place in the European Champions' League. Indeed, with seven points separating them from Manchester United, and Newcastle due to play at Old Trafford two days later, the Championship was a mathematical possibility for them, too.

Slaven Bilic, a key member of Croatia's national team who had been in English football for 15 months, had not played against Shearer before. The striker was absent through injury when Croatia drew 0–0 against England at Wembley in April 1996, and again when West Ham drew 1–1 at Newcastle in the Premiership seven months later. He had seen him often enough on TV, though, and had had plenty of discussions about him with his West Ham colleagues. Among these was 19-year-old Rio Ferdinand – cousin of Les – Shearer's Newcastle striking partner, who trained with the

England squad during Euro 96 and faced Shearer in practice matches. So Bilic took the view that he knew virtually all there was to know about his opponent; an attitude that was very much prevalent in West Ham's general preparations for the match.

It has often been said that, by stopping Shearer, a team can go a long way towards nullifying his side. It was interesting to note that in West Ham's preparations for the game – their deliberations on how best to tackle Newcastle – Shearer's name was not mentioned anywhere near as prominently as you might have anticipated. West Ham's manager, Harry Redknapp, took the view that Newcastle, with the likes of Ferdinand and Faustino Asprilla in their ranks, had a variety of sparkling scoring options and that to focus too intently on one man could only leave his team vulnerable to the skill of others.

To Redknapp, it was essential that his team adopt a positive attitude, that they concentrate on expressing their own attacking ability in the normal way. Even Shearer, he reasoned, can be reduced to the status of a mere mortal if his team are put under enough pressure to prevent them giving him the service he needs.

The day before the game, Redknapp, looking surprisingly relaxed in his small office at West Ham's Chadwell Heath training ground, explained: 'I wouldn't overemphasise Newcastle's strengths – if they have a weakness, it's at the back, so I think you have to attack them. There's no point in my telling our defenders to watch Shearer; they know they've got to watch him, just the same as they know they've got to watch Ferdinand. If I stress it, it's only going to put negative thoughts in their head or panic them.' Referring to West Ham's defensive system – they used three central-defenders, with Bilic and Ferdinand flanking centre-half Richard Hall – Redknapp continued: 'Liverpool didn't change their system [the same as West Ham's] when I saw them play Newcastle a few weeks ago, and although Newcastle scored three [in a 4–3 defeat], Liverpool murdered them, really.

'It's difficult to legislate for someone like Shearer because he can score goals from any position, can't he? He can get them with his head, he can get them from 25 to 30 yards, he can get them in the six-yard box – there's no telling where he's going to score from. He's just a goal machine. But I think we have enough ability and experience at the back with Richard, Slaven and Rio, to be able to deal with things. Between the three of them, they should be able to kill the ball down the channel that Shearer likes to spin on to. I would be expecting one of them to be blocking the channel before the ball gets there – you know, if the ball is being played by the right-back, I would be looking for our left-side central-defender to be in that left-hand channel to deal with it. As I said, I have no fears about the three of them not coping.'

Redknapp's attitude towards Shearer and Newcastle – his insistence on keeping a sense of perspective – was echoed by the men with the job of providing the manager with assessments of Newcastle's strengths and potential weaknesses in their previous matches. This exercise was carried out initially by West Ham's North-east scout Ian Hughes, who provided reports on New-castle's 3–1 home wins over Chelsea on 16 April (when Shearer scored twice) and Derby County on 19 April (when he got their first goal). These were passed to West Ham's chief scout Ted Pearce, who did a final check based on Newcastle's 1–0 win at Arsenal – through a Robbie Elliott strike – three days before their Upton Park visit.

Neither man could hardly fail to mention Shearer in his report. But the main references to Shearer could be found in the simple diagrams Hughes and Pearce provided on Newcastle's set-piece moves. One showed Shearer, taking a direct free-kick on the left, striking the ball right-footed to the top right corner of the goal; another depicted an indirect free-kick from the right by Asprilla, with Shearer attempting to get a touch by the near post, Ferdinand and Darren Peacock on the middle and Steve Watson by the far post.

As far as Shearer in open play was concerned, Ian Hughes noted: 'Ferdinand and Shearer often go into wide positions, with neither favouring one side in particular. Ferdinand experienced some difficulties in both games with his first touch on his left side, and was barracked by the fans. Although he did score in the Derby game, he poses more of a threat in the box in the air than on the ground. Shearer worked incredibly hard, always chasing to put defenders under pressure. His qualities need no comment. Suffice to say he is back to his best, and looks to get the ball to his feet in and around the penalty area, where he can turn defenders and get free-kicks.' The view was endorsed by Ted Pearce, who added: 'Ferdinand is very difficult to contain in the air when they hit him early. Shearer's runs must be watched from this situation.'

As for the service to Shearer, both Hughes and Pearce stressed the way Newcastle's team had changed under Dalglish. Hughes wrote: 'Newcastle are more defensively minded now, and play in a less flamboyant manner.' Pearce, referring to their performance against Arsenal, added: 'Newcastle's build-up was often slow and laboured. The full-backs rarely, if ever, get in advance of the ball, and only closely support attacks from the rear when the attack is well established.'

Having digested all the general information on Newcastle, the next step for Pearce and Redknapp was to work out what system or team 'shape' Newcastle would adopt. Against Arsenal, Newcastle had started the match in a 4-3-1-2 pattern, with Barton, Peacock, Watson and John Beresford at the back, Robert Lee, David Batty and Elliott in midfield; Asprilla in the 'hole' in front of them; and Shearer and Ferdinand at the front. But Pearce felt that Newcastle looked 'more balanced and generally more comfortable' as a result of the 52nd-minute substitution of Northern Ireland winger Keith Gillespie for Asprilla, which meant Gillespie operating on the right side of midfield and Newcastle switching to 4-4-2. 'Don't be surprised if Newcastle play 4-4-2 on Tuesday,' Pearce concluded. 'I think that's the system that Dalglish would want to play.'

Redknapp later admitted that this had concerned him. West Ham's system was 3-4-1-2 (Bilic, Hall, Ferdinand; Steve Potts, John Moncur, Steve Lomas, Stan Lazaridus; Hugo Porfirio; Paul

Kitson, John Hartson), and the manager said: 'I thought that Newcastle would give us a problem if they played 4–4–2 because they would have had four players in that midfield area, in tight, whereas two of our four [the wing-backs Potts and Lazaridus] are in the wider positions.' In view of the scoring potential of Shearer and Ferdinand, he was also uneasy about Gillespie's ability to get behind defences on the right and produce crosses. 'Lazaridus [the player who would be opposing Gillespie] is really an attacking player and doesn't have that many defensive qualities,' Redknapp explained. 'With Gillespie being supported by Barton, I envisaged our being caught one against two down that side.'

As it turned out, Newcastle named Gillespie as a substitute, Ferdinand failed a late fitness test on an ankle injury, and Newcastle started with virtually the same shape as West Ham – a 3–5–2 formation comprising Watson, Peacock, Albert; Barton, Clark, Elliott, Batty, Beresford; Shearer, Asprilla. 'I was very pleased when I got their team sheet,' Redknapp recalls.

'If you follow matches on TV or radio,' Pearce says, 'you will often hear the commentator talking about teams "cancelling each other out". That's because they have done their homework on each other. It's a bit like a game of chess. When you talk about what might have concerned us when we watched Newcastle, you've got to turn it on its head and also look at what concerned them about us. They would have had a guy at our game the previous Saturday [when West Ham crushed Sheffield Wednesday 5–1], and that performance will have influenced the way they played against us. It prompted Newcastle to do what we wanted them to do.'

This would probably not have happened had Keegan still been in charge. Keegan's first priority was to win every match, whereas with Dalglish, the first aim was not to lose. The match at West Ham underlined the differences between the two men perfectly. Newcastle did attack West Ham when they had the opportunity, but the reins were on. Instead of taking the gamble of all-out attack in a bid to gain the three points that would have kept Newcastle's Championship dreams alive, Dalglish was content to address himself to what was required to achieve the more realistic target of second place. The other way of putting it is that Dalglish played an ultra-professional percentage game, not dissimilar to the one Blackburn operated when he and Ray Harford were in command there, and it was to pay off for him.

Although Manchester United clinched the title that night (a result not just of Newcastle's failure to win at West Ham but also of Liverpool's 2–1 defeat at Wimbledon), Newcastle went on to claim the runners-up spot.

In the meantime, Slaven Bilic, who went on to help steer West Ham to Premiership safety, could only marvel at the extent to which Alan Shearer's teams tend to rely on him. 'He is very strange,' Bilic said the following day. 'I mean, when I compare him with the other strikers I have played with or against, I have to say he is not that skilful, he is not that quick and he is not that good in the air. I was probably more anxious about the possibility of playing against Ferdinand last night because Ferdinand can easily out-run you and he can murder you in the air. But Shearer has a little bit of everything and you know that even if he is having a quiet game he is always going to be there to score the goal.

'He will punish your every mistake. It doesn't matter how tiny it is, he will be there to punish it. He's unbelievable.'

CHAPTER ELEVEN

The Future

Unbelievable? To those who doubted Alan Shearer's ability to become one of the world's most respected football superstars, the word was never more appropriate than it was when he continued the sparkling form he'd shown in Euro 96 – this time, with the added responsibility of being England's captain.

Glenn Hoddle, having become Shearer's third manager at this level, and immediately faced with the challenge of lifting England above Italy, Poland, Moldova and Georgia in their qualifying group for the 1998 World Cup finals in France, did not take long to recognise that Shearer's potential could be exploited further. With England's Euro 96 captain Tony Adams and his predecessor David Platt both unavailable because of injury, Hoddle appointed Shearer to lead the side in his very first match in charge, the opening World Cup qualifying tie against Moldova in Chisinau on 1 September 1996. Any fears that the responsibility might have an adverse effect on his performance were dispelled by a 3–0 England victory in which he scored his first-ever international away goal; and again in the next tie against Poland at Wembley on 9 October, when he scored both goals in a 2–1 win.

Shearer missed the match in Georgia on 9 November – when Adams led England to a 2–0 victory – but with both men available for England's clash with Italy on 12 February 1997, Hoddle was now faced with the tricky business of having to choose between them for the captaincy. Hoddle, though, made his mind up early, and made his decision public a week before the game. 'There are certain players who may not be the best players or in the best positions to be captain, but you have them because of the other things they bring – the respect of the opposition, of referees, of teammates,' he said. 'I can remember Johann Cruyff playing for Holland, Diego Maradona for Argentina, Michel Platini for France. They were the players the opposition were scared of and they were made captain because of it. In a similar way, Eric Cantona has been made captain of Manchester United. Different reasons, perhaps, but the same principle. At international level, I think it is even more important than it is at club level. There is something special about leading your country and it should fall to special players. Alan is in that category, so you give him the armband and hope it gives him even greater power.'

It did not work out that way against Italy. Not fully fit and in an England line-up in which he had to rely on the enigmatic Matthew Le Tissier as his main source of front-line support, Shearer struggled to make an impression on the Italian defence. Italian teams have long been acknowledged as masters of the art of frustrating opposing strikers, especially when they are protecting a lead. Thus, even when Shearer was given a more orthodox striking partner in the 60th minute, through the substitution of Les Ferdinand for Le Tissier, England's chances of cancelling out Gianfranco Zola's first-half strike became increasingly remote.

However, by the end of Hoddle's first 12 months in charge – a period covering 11 matches – Shearer had every reason to believe that his career at international level was continuing to blossom. The other four matches in which he played – against Georgia, Poland, France and Brazil – brought him a further three goals, thus giving him an overall record of 16 in 34 games, and the honour of leading England to victory (at the expense of Italy, France and Brazil) in the close-season Tournoi de France.

One message to emerge from all this was that, notwithstanding the international potential of Manchester United's Paul Scholes, Shearer was still most likely to be at his best when he had Teddy

Sheringham as his partner, and vice versa. It came as no surprise that when Sheringham announced his intention to leave Tottenham, it immediately sparked speculation that he would be transferred to Newcastle, with Spurs taking Ferdinand in exchange. Most of Newcastle's Premiership rivals must have been relieved when Sheringham eventually went to Manchester United instead. Only in one of the four matches in which Hoddle was able to use Shearer and Sheringham together – the 1–0 defeat by Brazil in the Tournoi de France – did either or both fail to score. They were both on the mark in the 2–0 win over Georgia at Wembley in April and the 2–0 victory over Poland in Chorzow in May, and it was a Shearer goal from a Sheringham pass that gave them their 1–0 victory against France (and enabled them to clinch the Tournoi de France trophy) in Montpelier in June.

Glenn Roeder, who spent the season closely attached to the England camp as a part-time member of Hoddle's scouting and training team, says: 'In an ideal world, I think Alan would prefer to play against a team who push up to squeeze the play, because he's so good at timing his runs and exploiting that space behind them. He hasn't got that space when teams defend deeper as most of the Continental sides do, and that's when he needs people who can give him the ball early and accurately enough for him to just get in the finishing touch.

'Teddy's a good foil for Alan because he's very much the opposite of him. Whereas Alan is so much more effective when he is facing the goal, Teddy's strength is in playing with his back to the net. Teddy's ability to bring other people into the game is superb. I'm not just talking about his ability to bring Alan into the picture – I'm also talking about the way he will find other players, especially those in wide areas. When Alan scores from an early cross, you can bet that Teddy will have been involved in helping to set up the opportunity.'

The other message to emerge from Shearer's first season as an England player under Hoddle is that he has become very much a marked man in international football. This was emphasised particularly forcibly in England's last Tournoi de France clash, the 1–0 defeat against Brazil. The world champions did not stand on ceremony in the way they approached Shearer, who was flattened every time he looked as if he might threaten the Brazilian goal. Indeed, for Shearer, the contest was a far more difficult physical and technical ball game than just about anything he had previously experienced in an England shirt. He had only one goal attempt, a free-kick, in the entire 90 minutes.

He was not helped by the problems of the men behind him. In this way, the pattern of their performance was set at the start, with England hemmed into their own penalty area for what seemed an eternity. As Hoddle said later: 'There was a lot of fatigue out there from my players. They looked tired. I'm pleased with the way we passed the ball but we didn't get the balance right between our defending and our creative play. We did not get forward enough to support Alan Shearer.'

More disturbing was the reported verbal warning delivered to Shearer by Brazil's captain, Dunga: 'If you stop Shearer, there is a good chance England will not win the game. That is what we did and he will have to live with that kind of treatment in the World Cup. His reputation is big but he must prove he can take on the best and score goals in a World Cup. There was a lot of talk about Shearer and Ronaldo before the game. Neither scored, but with Ronaldo there is always the chance of that bit of magic. Has Shearer got it? It's a big question for him next year.'

This, of course, has since been overtaken by another question – that of whether Shearer will be in the England team by then. The broken right leg and damaged ankle ligaments he suffered in the Umbro Cup match against Chelsea at Goodison Park before the start of the 1997–98 season, when he stretched for a pass by David Batty and caught his studs in the grass, was a massive personal setback. The double injury, arguably the most worrying of his career, was expected to keep him out of action for virtually the entire domestic season. In view of his previous injuries – and especially the right knee cruciate ligament damage he suffered at

Blackburn – it also raised fears that he will never be quite the same player again. Even for Alan Shearer, there has to be a limit to how much punishment your body can take.

It's what's in the mind that's most important, however, which leads us to the observation that Shearer, now a man wealthy beyond his wildest dreams, might find it difficult to keep driving himself. Last season it was reported that, in addition to his Newcastle earnings, his personal commercial deals – including endorsement contracts with Umbro, Lucozade and Braun shavers – could be worth as much as £10 million to him. He was poised to move into a palatial home, complete with swimming-pool, on Sir John Hall's Wynyard Estate in Northumberland – a far cry from the modest Gosforth home in which he was brought up – and was widely believed to be in a position where he could retire tomorrow, with no financial worries for the rest of his life.

That situation can play strange tricks on a man's sense of commitment and dedication to a cause such as putting the ball in the net. Those close to the player in the North-east, however, insist that these characteristics are much too deeply ingrained in Shearer ever to be diluted or lost. This is certainly what comes across when you discuss his future with his professional colleagues. Glenn Roeder says: 'The first thing that struck me about Alan when I watched him in training for England was that he was no different to the way he was when I played against him for Newcastle and he was at the start of his career at Southampton. He did not score against me, but for 90 minutes he did not give me a moment's peace. I know it's easy to be enthusiastic about the game when you're 18 or 19, but his determination and will to win that day were exceptional. This side of Alan comes through just as strongly to me now in the England set-up. I honestly don't think that it's possible for him to train or play at 75 per cent – he is the type of person who has to give 100 per cent all the time.'

As Martine Delamere indicated in her observations about Shearer at the start of this book, this is a characteristic that would apply to Shearer in any field. So, once he ceases to be one of

Europe's most awesome goal machines, you can bet that the word 'unbelievable' will continue to be considered virtually his middle name.